My Journey of Discovery

*A Personal Testimony of
the Grace and Goodness of God.*

by
Zeph. R. Edwards

World rights reserved. This book or any portion thereof may not be copied or reproduced in any form or manner whatever, except as provided by law, without the written permission of the publisher, except by a reviewer who may quote brief passages in a review.

The author assumes full responsibility for the accuracy of all facts and quotations as cited in this book. The opinions expressed in this book are the author's personal views and interpretations, and do not necessarily reflect those of the publisher.

This book is provided with the understanding that the publisher is not engaged in giving spiritual, legal, medical, or other professional advice. If authoritative advice is needed, the reader should seek the counsel of a competent professional.

Copyright © 2017 Zeph R. Edwards

Copyright © 2017 Aspect Books, Inc.

ISBN-13: 978-1-4796-0786-0 (Paperback)

Library of Congress Control Number: 2017905482

Dedication

This book is dedicated to my wife Cindy,
and our sons Eliot and Sean.

Acknowledgements

This book is the product of what God has been doing in my life. I am especially grateful to Angela Misselhorn and Jill Smuda, teachers at Crest Lane SDA Elementary School, who first read the manuscript and gave me their honest impressions. Through his testimony, Randy Fishell of the Review and Herald Publishing Association caused me to catch the vision for the work necessary to bring this book to fruition. I thanked Randy for his editorial skills and wise suggestions in his revision of the manuscript. This book was formed in my heart before it was typed on paper. God used many friends to encourage me in the writing of this book. I also want to thank my family. My wife Cindy, is a treasure and a gift from the Lord. Also our children Eliot and Sean, who are a blessed heritage from the Lord. Finally, I thank God for His gracious leading in writing this book. The Holy Spirit gave me the desire to write my testimony. Our loving Father initiated it and completed it. I give Him the glory for whatever blessings may come from this book.

Table of Contents

Introduction………………………..……………………..……..7

The Early Years………………………………………………....9

Andrews University—Michigan…………….....………..…...19

Living in the Washington D.C. Metropolitan Area..................…..38

Medical School in the Dominican Republic…………………..…..47

From Pennsylvania back to Maryland……………….……….57

Travel and Challenges…………………………………………78

Reflections………………………………...………………….....92

The Journey Continues………………….….................…..100

A Joyful Celebration………………………...…………...108

Calvary: The Greatest Miracle……….................……..…..115

Introduction:

The purpose and intent of this story is to tell of the Lord's amazing grace and goodness in my life. The experiences that I have encountered are not uncommon to the human condition. To me the events that transpired were dreams that I had hoped and desired to achieve. The courage and the willingness to try and risk everything were based on the surety of my faith in the Almighty Creator, His holy word and his actions in my life and in human history.

Chapter one deals with my early experiences as a child and young adult, and the struggles I encountered. Chapter two concerns my attendance at Andrews University in Berrien Springs, Michigan. This experience represents the aspiration and achievement of certain goals and dreams, and serves as an example and metaphor of my testimony.

Chapter three addresses the issues of relocation and life in Washington D.C. Metropolitan Area. In chapter four, I discussed the challenge and ordeals of living and attending medical school in the Dominican Republic, returning to the United States, and working as a religious literature sales representative with the Pennsylvania Conference of Seventh-day Adventist. In chapter five my family and I were engaged in the process of moving from Pennsylvania back to our home state of Maryland in search of work. It also contains the story of our trip to the United Kingdom and the death of my father. Chapter six captures the account of our travels to Hawaii, an automobile accident, the death of my mother and the

Lord's deliverance from a debt of $53,000. In chapter seven, I pause and reflect on the nature and goodness of God's divine grace.

Chapter eight is an account of Cindy and me travelling to the G.C. convention in Atlanta, GA. We travelled to Michigan for her mother Natalie's birthday. I also traveled to the Caribbean to attend a convention. Cindy and I traveled to England for my niece's wedding, and then to Williamsburg, VA for our 40th wedding anniversary. Cindy was admitted to the hospital for surgery. In chapter nine, Cindy and I visit our son Sean in Maui, HI and celebrate our 41st wedding anniversary. In chapter 10, I reflect on Christ's supreme sacrifice in behalf of humanity and the entire universe.

Zeph R. Edwards

Chapter One
The Early Years

"There is a tide in the affairs of men, which taken at the flood, leads on to fortune, omitted, all the voyage of their life is bound in shallows and in miseries. On such a full sea are we now afloat: And we must take the current when it serves, or lose our ventures." —William Shakespeare, *Julius Caesar*, act 4, scene 3

One of the most remarkable events of my young life was the experience of a hurricane in 1954. The schools were closed! Many people boarded up their homes, businesses and shelters and secured their domestic and farm animals! Most of the week before the hurricane struck, was dark and cloudy, with rain and lightening. The day before the storm there was an eerie calm, with somber and overcast skies. Everyone were hunkered down in preparation for the coming tempest! We tried to get some sleep that night! At about 12:00 mid night or 1 am, the wind and rain picked up in intensity!

The rain came hard and the wind howled and screamed as a pack of wolves! The later it got, the more the wind whistled and boomed like a jet plane taking off on a giant runway! The whole house shook violently. The rafters on the roof were flapping noisily. The wind was violent and the rain was beating down with piercing furry. No one slept! We clung to each other and prayed for the break of day to come! When morning came, we discovered that the roof was leaking and other parts of the house were damaged. We all got some clothes and blankets and walked over to a relative's house, not far from where we lived, and weathered the rest of the receding storm, but especially for safety's sake, because our house was damaged. The morning after the hurricane passed, many houses, businesses and property were damaged or destroyed as a result of the storm. We were thankful to the Lord for saving our lives and that the damage to our house was not more widespread!

My father moved me from my grandparent's home and took me to live with his aunt (my grandmother's sister) Mrs. Jupiter Stewart and her family. We lived in the city of Saint James, Trinidad. I attended St. Agnes elementary school. These were wonderful years! I learned to appreciate music, education, faith and family life. Church life was happy and very family centered. Nine family members lived in the home. I believe that my father thought that this family situation will be better suited for my growth and development. Two of my cousins became school teachers, one was an attorney at law, another a business man and the others pursued profitable careers. I had good role models and a rich environment to encourage me to aspire and achieve my dreams. After completing my elementary education, I did not attend high school immediately. I worked at different occupations in order to support myself. I worked as a restaurant and hotel waiter and construction worker with my mother's brother, my uncle Colis Ambrose.

A major turning point in my life came while I was attending baptismal classes at the Stanmore Seventh-day Adventist church in Port-of-Spain, Trinidad. My Bible instructor's name was Ms. Wiltshire. She was an unmarried lady who lived with her unmarried sister Millie in a big house in the town of Belmont, a suburb of Port-of-Spain, the capital city. There was a third sister, who was married and had a family. Her name was Mrs. Bascome. She had a son by the name of Horace.

Owing to my early preparation and religious upbringing, I was a diligent and perceptive student in the baptismal class. These qualities were recognized by Ms. Iris Wiltshire. She spoke to me more directly about my background and disposition. She inquired, "Zeph, you're doing well in your studies and responses during the classes. Have you always attended church?"

I responded, "I attended church most of my life, with a few missed periods in between."

"Zeph you have a fantastic memory, she observed, how did that happen?"

"My dad is a great believer in memorization," I confided. For example, when I was about eleven years old, he bought a book of English poetry (he loved the classics) and insisted that I memorized the entire small book of poetry, verbatim. I memorized almost all the poems in the book. My parents especially our mother, taught us children to commit to memory the "Our Father's Prayer", "The Ten Commandments", the 23rd Psalm", "The Beatitudes" and other passages of scripture.

Ms. Iris Wiltshire was truly impressed with my memory skills. She inquired, "you do have plans of going to high school, don't you?"

To this I replied "of course, but I'm not sure." I related to her my circumstances. My mom and dad were separated at the time. I was living with dad's cousin and her husband, and had to work to help with living expenses. Being 15 years old, I was beyond normal age for entrance into high school. She offered to pay for me to attend a private high school, if I was willing to go.

"Would you like to go to high school, if I'm willing to help you?" I could not believe my ears! Without thought or hesitation, I said, "Yes, of course!" I thank the Lord profusely for His providence and loving-kindness! I applied, was accepted, and September of that year, I started classes at Ideal High School in Port-of-Spain, Trinidad. I struggled with some of my classes, owing to instability in my home life. There were difficulties getting meals, school clothes, books, and transportation to and from school. When Ms. Iris Wiltshire saw the less than satisfactory performance of my report card, she was very surprised, to say the least. She felt that with my impressive memory and learning ability, I should have done much better with my studies. After making her aware of my home situation, she offered me another wonderful opportunity. She proposed, "how would you like to come and live with me and my sister Millie, in our home?" I could not believe my good fortune and once again, without thought or hesitation, I said, "yes, I would be delighted to accept your offer!" After talking to my father and cousin Violet and her husband about the matter, I was allowed to go and live with Iris and Millie Wiltshire. Throughout my life, I thank the Almighty Creator for providing one of the most important opportunities of my life.

The day of my baptism in the Seventh-day Adventist church was a very special day. The ceremony was conducted by Pastor Charles Manoram of the Stanmore avenue church. The baptism ceremony was held at the Woodbrook Seventh-day Adventist church. While attending church at Stanmore avenue S.D.A. church I met and befriended a wonderful Christian family—the Maitlands. Bob and Alicia Maitland had 5 children: Monica, Louise, Carlyle, Lester, and Wendy Maitland. The friendship and kindness of this family meant more to me than they could ever know, even though I've expressed my gratitude to them several times and in tangible ways. Many times after leaving school, I was allowed to leave my books at their house. Their house was close to the high school I attended. Leaving several of my books at the Maitland's home, and not having to carry extra school books a great distance, was a tremendous help. I had to travel at least one hour before I arrived at my home in the city of Diego Martin. Many times they offered me a meal and good advice and counsel. The Maitland family members were good role models. I was especially impressed with the academic accomplishments of Carlyle Maitland. The Maitland's household was like my second home. This was definitely another provision from the Lord.

I do not recall exactly how I met the famous David Moore. He lived with his family in Woodbrook, Trinidad. He was the only one in his family that attended the S.D.A. church. He attended Osmond high school. David had many conflicts and expressed sentiments of self-doubt and lack of confidence. I tried to encourage him to have a more positive attitude towards life in general and his Christian walk in particular. David was a kind and gentle person.

The Early Years

I was a frequent visitor at his parent's home. He was one of the most original artist, I have ever known. He produced breath taking scenes of nature, portraits, buildings, people in action and animals in their natural habitats. We had a mutual admiration for each other. Sometimes I found myself wishing that I was as artistically talented, educated, and had a stable family background as David had. He often told me that he wished that he possessed my deep moral and strong spiritual values. For a long time, I did not understand what he meant. I often wondered why he was so pessimistic and melancholy sometimes, even though he had the materialistic comforts of life. He visited some of my relatives with me. On one occasion we were travelling for most of the day, and it was getting to be night fall, and I thought that it would be best to get a good night sleep, and then continue my journey home the next day. I asked David if I can spend the night at his apartment, in as much as I had about 25-30 miles to travel that night before I arrived at my home. I was very surprised and disappointed when he said no he did not want me to spend the night in his apartment. I continued on my journey and got home very tired and late that night. He later apologized for his behavior, but never told me the real reason for his actions. For a long time, I thought that I may have said or did something terrible that may have upset David.

    Many years later I received a letter from David while I was living in Washington D.C.. It was many pages long. It brought tears to my eyes. After thanking me for my friendship and the Christian example I had been to him, he said that he was receiving treatment for pneumonia and may have HIV. He said that several times he wanted to tell me that he was a homosexual, but he could not bring himself to admit his secret to me. He then explained to me that this is the reason why he did not want me to spend the night at his apartment, many years ago, because of the fear of discovery. As a Christian, understanding this condition had been difficult for me. The Bible plainly states that this activity and behavior is sin and an abomination to God. His grace, love, and forgiveness are offered to every sinner and every human being. My friendship with David Moore gave me an insight and the capacity for acceptance of homosexuals as human beings who were created by God in the same way that every human being was created by God. This experience deepened my understanding of God's love and his desire that Christians must reflect this same love to others. We cannot accept sin, but we must accept sinners for whom Christ died.

Another character building experience occurred, when I became a member of the Pathfinder club (scouts) in our church. In Pathfinders there were meetings to attend and many required honors (badges) to fulfill. Some of the honors that I received were camping, various nature honors requiring knowledge and presentation about different trees, animals, rocks, the sun, moon, stars, and other planetary bodies. I also earned honors for volunteering in the community, neighborhood clean up projects, and nursing home visits. I met the requirements for biking, tying many different knots, and wilderness survival skills. I also fulfilled the requirements for the swimming and boating honors.

While attending high school I worked at different part-time jobs in the catering industry—mainly as a waiter in hotels and restaurants. I had mixed feelings about working in this industry. Even though I did not get a large salary, I made lots of tips and met many different and interesting people. I liked this aspect of the job. I had cognitive and moral conflicts about working as a bartender. I served people liquor and other spirits, even though I've always been a teetotaler. It was part of my job, but I still felt that I was doing something wrong. I also engaged with many people who had little or no moral scruples regarding their personal deportment. I worked and saved quite a good sum of money because I was hoping and planning to emigrate to the United States to further my education. The Lord favored me with His providence when I received the wonderful news that I was granted a visa to travel to the US. This was a dream that came through! After saying goodbye to family members and friends, I made the historic trip to the U.S. in 1968.

Most of the trip went well, until we arrived at J.F.K. International Airport in New York. When we changed planes in Miami, Florida, our luggage was not transferred to the aircraft that took us to New York. Pan American Airlines took the affected passengers to a hotel by limousine services. I never knew such a large car existed, let alone rode in one! Of course, there were no financial obligations involved, because Pan AM was responsible for the snafus. The next day, our luggage arrived from Miami, and we were taken to La Guardia Airport. From there, the passengers were flown to our various destinations. My flight was bound for Reagan airport, Washington D.C. This was a time of anxious anticipation for me. While I was in New York, I contacted (phoned) uncle Arthur, my mom's brother, and informed him of my itinerary. I have not seen him for many years and was not absolutely sure what he looked like. As we landed, I made my way to the immigration check point. After this process was completed, everyone proceeded to the baggage area to collect their luggage. I collected my two suitcases and made my way to the reception area. I began scanning the crowd for Uncle Arthur. After a while, I saw a moderately tall, medium built, middle aged man walking towards me. I knew it was him, because he resembled my mom. "Zeph, is that you? I'm your Uncle Arthur. How was your trip?" He reached out and took one of my two suitcases.

"The flight from Trinidad to Miami, Florida and to New York was long but enjoyable. Even though our bags were left in Miami, Florida, everything turned out well. As we walked towards his car, we continued our conversation.

"What's your impression of America so Far?"

"I'm amazed at how large everything is, and how much in a hurry everyone was. I rode in the largest car (limousine) I've ever seen in my life. The streets were the broadest and the buildings were the largest I've ever seen. I don't understand how a building as tall as the Empire State building does not topple and fall when strong winds blow." We finally reached the parking lot where he parked his car. We placed the luggage in the trunk, and started on our way to his home in Seat Pleasant, Maryland. We continued our conversation in the car.

"Tell me about the family back home, how are they doing?"

"My mom and dad are well and doing fine, so are my brothers and sisters. After being sick with an abdominal disease, for some considerable length of time, Aunt Ruth (Uncle Arthur's sister) went to be with the Lord." We talked about other members of the family for the duration of the trip home to Seat Pleasant, Maryland.

The ensuing days, weeks, months were full of adjustments-dietary, cultural, linguistic and logistical. Owing to the busy professional lives of my uncle and his wife, Pam (a nurse), they did not make home cooked meals everyday, like I'd grown accustomed to having. I got in the habit of eating cereals and cooking my own meals. The changing of the seasons were a major item. I've always known spring and summer seasons. I had to learn and adjust to autumn and winter as well. Winter was by far the hardest season I'd had to deal with. I'd never seen real snow and had no experience of how to live and deal with it. However, with the proper clothes, encouragement from family and acquaintances, and a good attitude, I adjusted and actually grew to like and enjoy the winter season. The fact that Christmas time is my favorite time of the year, greatly helped in my process of adjustment. I'd always spoken English, therefore I had no difficulty understanding the language. However, my English was from a British background and emphasis. There were challenges with some intonations and pronunciations. However, with practice and public speaking, almost all difficulties with accentuation were resolved with the passing of time. In school, at all levels, I excelled in English and all literary courses.

The matter of transportation was another area of difficulty and challenge. In 1968, I did not yet have my driver's license. I signed up with the Easy Method Driving School, and after several lessons, I successfully acquired my Maryland driver's license. This was one of the happiest days of my life!

The Early Years

Owing to the fact that I had some difficulty acquiring my high school transcripts from Trinidad, I was required to take the GED course. Instead of doing that, I purchased a book that prepares one for the test. I studied the book, took the GED test, and passed without difficulty. I gave thanks and praise to the Lord for his goodness!

For some time, I gave serious thought to a career and future endeavors. This opportunity came, when uncle Arthur helped me to qualify for the Certify Laboratory Assistant course that was taught at Washington D.C. General Hospital. This was a federal government program, twelve months in duration, that I did not have to pay for. The course included Hematology, Blood Banking, Chemistry, Microbiology, Bacteriology, Urinalysis, and Phlebotomy. This was a hard and trying experience, but by God's grace, I was able to complete this year-long course. This experience placed me on a successful pathway of accomplishment. I want to emphasize my thankfulness and gratitude to uncle Arthur for his kindness, encouragement, and advocacy on my behalf. He contributed greatly to my growth, development, and success.

While I was doing the clinical laboratory course at Washington D.C. General hospital, Ms. Virginia (Gene) Ross, who taught bacteriology and microbiology, was of enormous help and encouragement to me. She accepted another job offer and left the program when I was about three quarters of the way to finish. I did not know who her new employer was. As a result I lost track of her whereabouts. After graduating from the medical technician course, I worked as a part-time phlebotomist at several different clinics and hospital facilities. I came to understand that Ms. Virginia Ross was the evening supervisor of the clinical laboratory at Children's Hospital National Center. I paid her a visit and she gave me a job in the laboratory. This was my first full-time job as a laboratory technician. Without question, this opportunity was made possible by my Heavenly Father. I worked in three (3) different parts of the laboratory. I worked in hematology, blood banking, (immunohematology) and urology (urinalysis).

This job was a blessing on several levels. It greatly expanded my knowledge and experience in the field of medical technology. It was the highest paid income I'd ever received. I established a good savings account, I rented my first apartment, and purchased my first used car, a 1965 Ford Falcon. I started my college education at Prince George's Community College, in Largo, Maryland. During this period of time, I met and started dating a young lady by the name of Debbie Watkins. Her last name changed after she was subsequently married. After attending Prince George's Community College for 2-1/2 years, I decided to transfer to Andrews University in Berrien Springs, Michigan.

Chapter 2

Andrews University—Michigan

"I already know the plans I have for you. I will help you, not hurt you. I will give you a future and a hope." —Jeremiah 29: 11 (The Clear Word)

When I made the decision to continue my education, I chose to attend Andrews University in Berrien Springs, Michigan. This is a Christian institution of higher learning and a world-class University as well. Andrews University epitomizes and illustrates the reason for my story—the promise and reality of faith and hope in the aspiration and achievement of my goals and dreams. To have the opportunity to learn, work, play and live with scholars and people from different parts of the world, with whom I share similar beliefs, principles and values have been a very moving experience for me. Every teacher and event was dedicated to the success of the learning process. As I interacted with my professors and fellow students, I was invited to dinner, and fellowshipped in the homes of several faculty members. In these settings I saw how my teachers interacted with their family members as well as students in an informal way. On-campus and off-campus retreats and activities were laboratories, where long term relationships were formed, and effective learning experiences transpired.

As a person who came from a modest background and a broken family, to have the opportunity to attend a private institution of higher learning such as Andrews University never entered my imagination as a young child. I hoped and dreamed of attending and finishing high school. This was the extent of my aspiration, as far as formal education was concerned. I knew that I had to get out in the real world, find a job, and earn a living. That is exactly what I did, until the hand of divine fate guided my life in pathways of inexpressible dreams and along the road of my uncommon journey of discovery.

In the fall of 1972, I drove from Washington D.C. to Andrews University in Berrien Springs, Michigan. I wondered if the Toyota Corolla would make the twelve hour trip from Washington D.C. to Michigan. The trip was pleasant and uneventful, and after driving for many hours and several stops along the way, I finally arrived at my destination safely. I went to the men's dormitory, Meiers Hall, and was given an assigned room. I was introduced to my roommate and got settled in. The next day I went to the administration building and registered in the pre-medicine curriculum and started classes. During that first year at Andrews University, the grades in my non-science classes were good, but I was not pleased with the grades in my science classes. I was involved in several extra-curricular activities on campus, and may have "spread myself too thinly," and as a result, did not excel as much as I wanted to.

One of the most significant events that occurred at the beginning of my first year at the University (I was a transfer student, after having completed a year of school at Prince George's Community College in Largo, Maryland) was the student retreat, at a place called Camp Michiana. The weekend, Friday evening to Sunday morning, was designed so that students and professors could become acquainted. There was a special speaker for the duration of the retreat. His name was Dr. Edward Heppenstall, Professor of Theology and Biblical Philosophy. At the time, he was teaching at Loma Linda University, in Loma Linda, California. The theme of his presentation dealt with knowing our true identity in Christ and the implication of this knowledge to success in life in general and to the academic experience in particular. The thesis and thrust of his thoughts and teachings was that all human beings are created in the image of a loving and almighty Creator, and the mission of our lives is to reflect His image, in the same way that Christ's life reflected the image of God, His father. Living this life is made possible by God's Holy Spirit, when we accept Jesus Christ as our personal Savior and Lord of our lives. I was fortunate to be able to spend some personal time with Dr. Edward Heppenstall. He was an Englishman—very learned, but quite affable and approachable. From him, I learned a deeper insight into the divine love of God. God's love is both just and merciful. His justice must be satisfied. He cannot compromise with sin (rebellion). Jesus died on the cross because God's law cannot be broken or changed. God's love also provided, through Jesus' death on the cross, full restoration as God's children for all those who accept Jesus Christ as their Savior and Lord.

It was in Dr. Joyce Rochat's English class that the thirst to write and give literary and creative expression to my thoughts and life experience came to fruition. In her class, I really learned the beauty of language and the power of words. I learned to better appreciate the poetry and majesty of Elizabethan English. Two of my favorite books are *The Merchant of Venice* by William Shakespeare and *Les Misérables* by Victor Hugo.

Among the many friends I was fortune to make while attending Andrews was Dorothy Caviness. We sat in a math class together. In conversation, I spoke to her of my friend Dave Buckman. Apparently she was impressed, and I also spoke to Dave about Dotty. After some time elapsed, they met, dated, and eventually married and had two girls—Jeannie and Ladelle—after Dave finished medical school at Loma Linda University.

Another dear and life-long friendship was that of Paul and Lenore Brantley, when we lived in the Washington D.C. metropolitan area in 1970. We attended Dupont Park church. They were teachers at Dupont Park church school. They took classes towards their master's degree in education at Washington D.C. Teachers College (later the University of the District of Columbia). We spent wonderful times together. I visited them when they lived in Columbus, Ohio, while Paul was doing his PhD, at Ohio State University. They also visited me while I was a student at Andrews University.

During the school year of 1973, I was involved in several activities at the university: the education reform committee, ACYA (Adventist Christian Youth in Action), Andrews University telephone "hot line" program, and other student activities. I had some very memorable times and events as a member of Adventist Christian Youth in Action (ACYA). This was a student organization that leaves the university on each Saturday by car or bus to different churches, schools, hospitals, or jails to sing and do instrumental music, preach and give personal testimony about our Christian experiences. This was a time of rich communion and fellowship with one another and others as well. There were between 15–20 members in the group. Sometimes we would go as one group, and other times we would go into two different groups, to different assignments. The people in the places we visited always expressed tremendous appreciation for the music, testimonies, and spoken word. We, the students, also received a wonderful blessing of affirmation and sense of value. Many life-long friendships were formed from this group. Several students found their spouses in the group. This was truly a special time in our academic experience.

At the end of that semester I was able to move out of Meier Hall, the men's dormitory, and into the community. I lived at the "White House." This was a big white house that was owned by Mr. & Mrs. Warren (Bud) and Charlotte Davis. The Davis family—Danny, Julie, Candy, Pat and Pam (twins) and Mary—lived on the first floor. Students lived on the second floor. My roommate's name was Dave Huber. He was a seminarian, preparing for the ministry. His girlfriend was a graduate student by the name of Joycelyn Scrooby from South Africa. There were about 5 or 6 other seminary students who lived at the "White House." I was the first and only undergraduate student, for some time, who lived there. I inherited the room from Barry Black, the famous Chaplain of the United States Senate. I knew members of Barry's immediate family: his mother, and his sisters Gloria and Beverly. The times I spend with Barry Black's family were wonderful and happy memories. His mom was articulate, kind, and spoke quickly. Both of his sisters that I knew were sensitive, courteous, and affable Christian young ladies. Barry's wife Brenda and his mother were his foundation and sources of his success. Of course our heavenly Father and Barry's extraordinary talents and abilities played a major role in his aspirations and achievements.

After living at the "White House" for some time, I started to date Julie Davis, the oldest daughter of Mr. & Mrs. Warren "Bud" Davis, the owner of the house. Julie was eighteen years old at the time. She was a warm and endearing Christian young lady of Caucasian background. She had five siblings: Danny, Candy, Pam and Pat (who were twins) and Mary, the youngest sibling. The entire Davis family was pleasant and comfortable to be around. After Julie and I dated for some time, I asked her to marry me. She loved me, however, because of circumstances, we decided that this may not be the best course to follow at that particular time. Although we did not marry, we shared many wonderful and memorable experiences together.

At the "White House" my room-mates were first Dave Huber, and sometime later my room-mate was Ken Kenittle, an undergraduate student at Andrews University. Another of my memorable suite-mates was Roger Dupree. He was attending school on the G.I. Bill. One semester, as we were talking about school, our classes and work schedule, I said, "I don't know if I'll be able to return to school next semester because I don't have enough money to pay for my classes for the present semester and for the next semester as well." Upon hearing this, Roger offered to give me over $350.00 from his G.I. check, in order to pay for my classes that semester. Initially, I refused his offer. "Roger," I said, "I won't be able to repay you this money!"

He responded, "I don't want it back, Zeph, I want you to be able to pay your tuition and return to school." With gratitude I accepted Roger's gift and thanked him sincerely.

When I was about eight or nine years old my father bought me a small harmonica. Over time, I learned to play the instrument quite well, mostly for my own enjoyment and pleasure. On many an occasion when I became frustrated, irritated, aggravated, or discouraged, I would play my harp, and it brought peace and solace to my heart, mind, and spirit. I also wanted to play the piano, the guitar, and violin, because I love music. However, as I grew older, only the harp stuck with me, so to speak! While I was a student in the dormitory at Andrews University, as was my custom I would play the harp for my enjoyment and peace of mind. As my roommates and suitemates heard the music, they were impressed and complimented me on my talent and skill. In time I received several requests to play for different public events. Initially, I was apprehensive, and recoiled at the prospect of performing before live audiences. After much encouragement from friends and other fellow students, I agreed to play at different events, on and off campus. This was the beginning of a long experience of musical performances.

I became involved in several aspects of student life at the University. I was a member of a student education reform committee. It's purpose was to explore ways and methods whereby the education process can be enhanced for the academic community in general and for the students in particular. The committee then submitted its findings and recommendations to the University dean for consideration. The committee was comprised of undergraduate, graduate, and faculty members of the University. This was a very exhausting and beneficial experience. I was involved in a volunteer phone counseling group that sought to reach out to people in the community with concern and support in their personal challenges and life struggles. I also took part in missionary activities—singing and performing for church groups, nursing home facilities, and penal institutions.

In the summer of 1973, I got a job as a clinical laboratory technician at Lee Memorial Hospital in Dowagic, Michigan about 15 miles east of Berrien Springs, MI. I worked in different sections of the laboratory—hematology, chemistry, urinalysis, and phlebotomy. I earned enough money that summer in order to return to school. I also made some new friends. One of the people I befriended was Arlene Mullet. She was a junior medical technology student at Michigan State University in East Lansing, MI. I shared with her my knowledge of medical technology—hematology, blood banking, urinalysis, and phlebotomy. We became good friends and had a wonderful time during the summer of 1973. As we parted to return to school at the two different universities that we attended, I bought her a record by the Carpenters and wrote her the following poem as a gift:

> "A Friend"
> A friend is one who cares a lot.
> A friend is one who shares his thoughts.
> A friend is one who feels and knows,
> The joys, the sorrows, and the woes,
> A companion sometimes doesn't show.
> I'm thankful for the friend you've been—
> your laughs, your smiles, your everything.
> I enjoyed the many things we've shared—
> your time, my books, and our ideas.
> Though you return to MSU,
> I shall still remember you.
> We may not meet in life again.
> If that's the way that fate intends,
> continue striving for your goal,
> and you'll find fulfillment for your soul.

Arlene Mullet returned to Michigan State University to finish her bachelor's degree in medical technology, and I returned to Andrews University. I never saw her again.

I registered for classes that fall of 1973. I also got a job on campus at the Berrien Springs Bindery. Classes, work, and campus activities were quite interesting and challenging. While working at the bindery, I met a certain young lady by the name of Cynthia Marie Bullock. I introduced myself: "Hi my name is Zeph Edwards, what's yours?" There was no answer! I continued. "I'm a sophomore pre-med student at Andrews, Do you attend school here also?" There was still no answer! After this experience, I thought that she probably was not a student at the university. I returned to my work of cutting the National Geographic magazines and stacking them on a shelf. One day of that same week, Cindy M. Bullock passed me in the bindery and said "hi" to me. That greeting made me feel better throughout that entire day. I felt a likeness to her, the very first time I saw Cindy Bullock. As time went on, we talked on a more regular basis.

During the semester, I continued to be involved with the student education reform committee, was the off-campus leader for student activities, and worked with the telephone "hot line" counseling program. Involvement with this program helped with my personal growth and development. I was able to talk with many different people, listen to their problems and life crises, and suggest options and solutions to their challenges. The following story is my most poignant experience while working with the "hot line" counseling program: The voice on the other end of the telephone said, "hello, I'm calling to say goodbye. I'm stepping off the world."

I said. "Stepping off the world? Where are you going?" listening intently, the man continued to speak.

"I'm no good! I can't keep a job! My wife and children don't respect me, because I can't live up to their expectations! What's the use? I'm gonna take my life and get it over with." I almost froze in fear, as I listened to this man, who from the tone and intensity of his voice, clearly intended to carry out his intentions. I prayed hard for guidance and wisdom in order to salvage this solution. I don't remember what I said exactly, but I spoke to this man an hour or more.

As I listened, I said, "It doesn't have to end this way! I would like you to give me a chance to help you, and if it doesn't work out, you can still go ahead with your plan to commit suicide, but please give me a chance to help you!" To my great surprise and relief, he agreed to my suggestion that he come into the University Counseling Center and talk with a counselor. I never knew this man's name. I glimpsed him for a brief moment as he came into the Counseling Center. He was a tall, husky, strawberry blonde-haired man. He appeared to be in his forties. I am disposed to believe that this man found the help that he so desperately needed, and continued to be a part of his family. However, I never saw or heard anything more about this man again. This incident and involvement in the "hot line" program had a marked and profound effect on my life. I was a biology, pre-med major in college. After this experience, I decided to change my major to psychology, pre-med, with the intention of becoming a clinical psychologist, as my second choice to becoming a medical doctor.

Working in the "hot line" program, located in the basement of the University campus center, provided an opportune setting for courting the girl that I was dating. We spent a lot of time together, while I was tending the telephone lines. We stole our first kiss while I was a volunteer in the program. Owing to my hectic schedule of classes and work, the time spent at the "hot line" program and weekends were about the only opportunities we had to spend some time together. After several months of dating, Cindy and I became engaged to be married at the end of the winter semester. Owing to financial and other circumstances we decided to go to the justice of the peace, and have a church wedding later.

A serious problem presented itself. Cindy could not find her birth certificate. She had not seen it since she was 7 or 8 years old. We decided to pray about the matter. We also felt that this would be a sign and test as to whether the Lord approved of our marriage. Cindy is Caucasian and I am of African-American background. The scripture teaches that believers (Christian) should not be unequally yoked with unbelievers. Cindy and I are both third generation Christian Seventh-day Adventists. Our spiritual beliefs, principles, values and faith are the same. I will never forget the day that I received that most important telephone call. "I found it! I found it!" I had to remove the phone from my ear, owing to her excitement. We were both elated and took this find as a positive affirmation form the Lord.

On May 20th, 1974, Cindy and I were married at the court house in St. Joseph, Michigan. We then drove back to Andrews University in Berrien Springs. Cindy returned to work at the bindery and I attended my classes as scheduled. We had not yet found an apartment, therefore Cindy continued to live at her parents' house while I lived at the "White House" with the seminary students. We eventually found our first apartment on Grove Street, close to the University. Cindy and I did not have to get married because of intimate physical contact. Our marriage was consummated after we were married.

In the summer of 1974, I got a job with the Michigan Conference of SDA to work as a security guard at the Michigan Camp Meeting in Grand Ledge, Michigan. This was a very interesting, challenging, and exciting time. We continued to search for an appropriate apartment close to the university. This was not an easy task, therefore my wife Cindy continued to live at her parents' home. We did not tell many friends that we were married. During the summer of 1974, I lived and worked in Grand Ledge, Michigan, while Cindy worked and lived in Berrien Springs, Michigan. We talked on the telephone, wrote each other letters almost every day, and took turns visiting each other on weekends. Everything went well until one day when I received a very disturbing telephone call! The voice at the end of the telephone line was Cindy's, my wife! "You've gotta come to Berrien Springs immediately! Debbie Paul, my best friend, said that she saw our marriage announcement in the local newspaper. I've got to get out of my parent's house, because I have not yet told them that we are married!" I told my supervisor that I had an emergency and I had to go to Berrien Springs immediately. I drove as fast as I could, and got into Berrien Springs in about forty-five minutes to one hour. The trip usually takes one hour and a half to two hours. There were many issues to address when I got into Berrien Springs. We found some temporary lodging with a couple, Mark and Rene, who were our friends. After settling most issues, I returned to work at Grand Ledge. We later found a small apartment on Grove Street, in Berrien Springs, that summer.

Owing to many family conflicts, misunderstandings, and trouble, Cindy and I decided to return to Maryland, where I planned to finish college at Washington Adventist University. I wrote the following letter to Cindy's parents and family with the hope of shedding light and understanding on a difficult situation:

> I am aware that there have been misunderstandings and perhaps hurt feelings concerning Cindy and I. I am very sorry that our marriage has caused such divisions and hurt feelings among your family and other relatives. I guess I didn't fully realize the kind of impact that our marriage had on your family. However, by your letters to Cindy, by our visits to Berrien Springs, and by Sylvia's visit here with us, I was better able to understand the way you think and feel about the situation. Before I proceed further I think that It's important to state the reason for writing this letter. First, let me say that I do not think that our marriage was a mistake, that is was a sin or that it was wrong in any way, therefore I'm not offering an apology. My purpose in writing this letter is to clear up any misunderstanding or misinformation concerning the situation. Also to try to find out what the Bible teaches and what should be the Christian attitude towards this matter. I know that situations like this are usually dealt with very emotionally. However, if we want to find satisfactory answers to the many questions we face, we must use reason, knowledge, understanding, and a study

of the scriptures to find out what it says (reads) concerning this matter.

I think that it is helpful and important for you to be acquainted with the manner in which my parents trained and reared me. My mother's father (my grandfather) was the pastor of the Seventh-day Adventist church that we attended. My father's family were Episcopalians before they became Adventist. My parents taught me that God is the Creator and sustainer of all human beings, plants, animals, and all other forms of life. However, He is especially the Father of all true Christian believers, His church. They (we) are all children of God and we are one family in Christ Jesus. The Bible also teaches this truth. This teaching was not only taught in words but it was practiced in our family and with fellow believers. In Latin America, we know nothing about black churches, white churches, Chinese churches or Indian churches. All Seventh-day Adventists worship together as the Christian believers did in the second chapter in the book of Acts. Seventh-day Adventists usually marry other S.D.A. that they happen to fall in love with. It did not matter if the S.D.A. member was Indian, African, Japanese, or a Caucasian believer. It was the same way among the Baptist, Episcopalians, Methodist, Presbyterians, or Lutherans. The Bible teaches that we should not be unequally yoked with unbelievers. It says nothing about race, nationality, or color. My wife could easily have been Chinese, Indian, or African-American. She just happened to be Caucasian. I've dated and was friendly with different girls. I've had girls ask me to marry them, white and black. However, they were not Seventh-day Adventist, therefore I could not marry them. My grandmother's grandfather was an Englishman. My uncle's (father's brother) wife was an East Indian. My mother's brother's (uncle) wife was an Englishwoman. They lived in Canada with their three children and grandchildren. I related these experiences to help you to understand the kind of background and environment in which I grew up. It was not until the 1960s when I came to the United States from Latin America that I became aware of the problem of color and race that existed in America, and in the S.D.A. Church. I thought that the situation was inhuman, sinful, and repugnant then, and I still feel the same way today.

The Bible, in the book of Acts, chapter 17, verse 26, states: "God hath made of one blood all nations of men for to dwell on all the face of the earth, and hath determined the times before appointed, and the bounds of their habitations." As a laboratory technician, I know this verse to be true. I have looked at the blood of all kinds of people under the microscope, and I have found that there is no difference in human blood. I also looked at the blood of dogs and horses, and there is a great difference. The blood of any living form or being is its life. A person can live with an artificial heart, lung, kidney, or just about any other organ of the body, perhaps someday medical science may be even able to do a successful brain transplant, but there is no adequate substitute for human blood.

I remember that sometime ago you wrote us a letter concerning statements that Ellen G. White made in her book *Selected Messages*, regarding mixed marriages. I will like to turn my attention to this matter at this time. I think you may be aware that some statements made by Mrs. White have been misused out of context by persons, and sad to say also by our own denomination. For instance, the books *Selected Messages*, volume 1 and 2, were compiled by the Ellen G. White Estate. When a book is compiled, there is always the chance that a passage and its full meaning can be taken out of context, and therefore is misunderstood. A little later in this letter I will try to show you what I mean. However, at this time, I would like to quote some statements made by Ellen White of which you may not be aware:

"No distinction on account of nationality, race, or caste, is recognized by God. He is the maker of all mankind. All men are of one family by creation, and all are one through redemption. Christ came to demolish every wall of partition, to throw open every compartment of the temple, that every soul may have free access to God... In Christ there is neither Jew nor Greek, bond nor free" (*Christ Object Lessons*, p. 386).

"The religion of the Bible recognizes no caste or color. It ignores rank, wealth, worldly honor. God estimates men as men. With Him (God), character decides their worth. And we are to recognize the Spirit of Christ in whoever it is revealed" (*Testimonies* Vol. 9, p. 223).

"The walls of sectarianism and caste and race will fall down when the true missionary spirit enters the hearts of men. Prejudice is melted away by the love of God" (*The Southern Work,* 1966 ed., p. 55).

"The Lord Jesus came to our world to save men and women of all nationalities. He died just as much for the colored people as for the white race... The Lord's eye is upon all His creatures. He loves them all, and makes no differences between white and black, except that he had a special, tender pity for those who are called to bear a greater burden than others... All are one in Christ. Birth, station, nationality or color cannot elevate or degrade men, the character makes the man. If a red man a Chinese or an African gives his heart to God, in obedience and faith, Jesus loves him none the less for his color. He calls him well-beloved brother...men may have both hereditary and cultivated prejudices, but when the love of Jesus fills the heart, and they become one in Christ, they will have the same spirit that he had" (*The Southern Work*, 1966 e., pp. 9-14).

Now I will like to turn my attention to the passage in *Selected Messages*, book 2, to which you referred in the past letter. These passages were written in 1896 and 1912, concerning the "inadvisability of interracial marriages, because of the prevailing circumstances and conditions that could result in controversy confusion and bitterness." I would strongly urge that you read the little booklet *The Southern Work*, by E.G. White, so that you will have a proper understanding of the circumstances and conditions that existed at the time she made those statements. Of course those statements would be valid as long as, and whenever or wherever, those conditions exist. Therefore, the questions should be, what kind of conditions existed in those days, and do those conditions exist today? I will address the first question first. After the American Civil War, passage of the Thirteenth Amendment to the constitution, in the year 1865, outlawed slavery in the United States; the Fourteenth Amendment gave this oppressed people the right to vote. In 1875, the law forbade discrimination in public places and in public transportation. However, things changed, and in 1883 the U.S. Supreme court ruled that the Civil

Rights Act of 1875 was unconstitutional, meaning that the Fourteenth Amendment protected only against infringement of civil rights by states, and not by private individuals. By 1910 every one of the former confederate states had disenfranchised its black citizens. This meant that the intolerable economic, political, and social conditions of the past had once again returned. I think that this should be enough information to give you a fair picture of the economic and social conditions that existed in those days. Mrs. White made the statements concerning this matter of inter-marriages in 1896 and 1912. Therefore, it would not only be wrong and dangerous, but cruel and inconsiderate for a couple to marry interracially during such times, anywhere in the United States— North or South. During those times, segregation, discrimination, and prejudice were the laws of the land.

Now let me address the second question. In 1954, in a landmark decision, the U.S. supreme court reversed itself and in effect stated that segregation and discrimination were wrong and unconstitutional. It took the Supreme Court 79 years to come to this decision. Even in the 1950s, the social climate was not the best for mixed marriages, although times were better than 79 years before. In 1964, the Civil Rights Act (law) dealt with many aspects of discrimination, including voting rights, public accommodations, and employment. Although there are still many problems among the races, I think you will agree that social and economic conditions are much different than they were 80 years before. Statistics show that most interracial marriages are much more stable than marriages between couples of same race.

Ellen White also made statements about other matters that had particular applications for the period of time in which she made them. She made statements concerning the city, the possessions of bicycles, about medication, dress reform, and other subject matters. I will be glad to discuss further any of these topics with you. You may ask the question as to whether most of what Ellen White said had application only for particular times or circumstances. My answer is no. Anything that is of a spiritual nature or is based on principle does not apply to particular times or circumstances, but is eternal in nature. For example, the Ten Commandments are timeless and eternal; human beings can have salvation only through Jesus Christ—that will never change. It is only by faith that we can please God. Other principles in the Bible read thus: "For where your treasures is, there will your heart be also". (Matt. 6:21). "For the living know that they shall die, but the dead know not anything" (Eccles. 9:5). These are basic unchangeable truths, belonging to all future generations as well as to the one to whom they were first given. The Bible counsels us to study to show ourselves approved unto God, so that we may not be ashamed, rightly dividing the word of truth.

In his book *The Genealogy of Ellen Gould Harmon White*, Dr. Charles Dudley made the following statement: "Following the disappointment (of 1844), God guided his people through three prophets who gave messages of assurances. Three spokespersons were William Foye, Hazen Foss (the brother-in-law of Mary Gould Harmon Foss, who was Ellen Gould Harmon's sister)—they were classified as negro or colored—and Ellen Gould Harmon. The Lord chose Ellen Gould Harmon to be his spokesperson and to guide the S.D.A. church through visions, dreams, and prophecies from 1846 to 1915, and until the end of time. Ellen Gould Harmon married a Caucasian gentlemen by the name of James S. White. Eunice, Ellen's mother, was a mulatto (mixed race): whose roots can be traced to New Jersey and the Caribbean. The roots of Robert Harmon, her father, were of the African, Moor, Nanticoke Indian, and English colored people living on the Eastern shores of Delaware.

There is much more I will like to say in this letter, but I believe that enough has been said for the present time. May the Lord richly bless the entire family. Give our regards to all and write soon. Bye.

For a great part of my life, the game of table tennis has been a great motivator and a source of satisfaction and comfort. Soccer was the game that first held that honor. However, during a game of soccer, the ball rolled into a patch of moderately high grass. I proceeded to kick the soccer ball out of the grass. There was a stone in front of the ball, but I did not see it. I kicked the stone instead of the ball. I injured the instep of my right foot. I was about fourteen years old. I gave up soccer and took up table tennis, mainly as a result of this injury. The game of table tennis has played an important part in my life. I like the game, and enjoy playing it. But the game has a wider application, regarding my academic achievements in particular and self-confidence about life in general. Before playing a game of table tennis, I would do a warm-up routine. I would jog around the track three or four times, and do a vigorous stretch routine for thirty minutes. This helped to get my body in shape—it prepared my body and mind for a good game of tennis. Similarly, in other aspects of my life, when I am prepared—I've prayed, think things through, and play carefully—I usually get a more desired out-come.

The concepts of preparation and focus were very important principles I learned while playing the game of table tennis. I applied these lessons and principles to my studies, and other goals and endeavors that I aspired to achieve. The game of table tennis did help me with my studies and my self-confidence, while I was a student at Andrews University. To have a relatively good chance for success (winning the game) I usually planned a short and long term strategy for the game. For example, is it better play an offensive or defensive game or both? It's a good tactic to spin the ball and keep it low. I always tried to keep my eyes on the ball, which determines how I responded and returned the ball. I tried my best to read my opponent's personality, to determine his or her approach to the game. Is he or she an aggressive or defensive player? Is he or she a cognitive or emotional player? This knowledge helped me to adjust my game accordingly. A vigorous game of table tennis is an excellent source of exercise and well-being. The game must be played fairly. To succeed, one must play to win. When I play the game of table tennis or the game of life, I play with the desire to win. Throughout my long experiences of playing table tennis, I've formed many short and long term friendships with people from Russia, China, Romania, South Korea, Latin America, as well as North America.

Chapter 3
Living in the Washington Metropolitan Area

"The Lord is my light and my salvation. Whom then shall I fear? The Lord is the strength of my life. Of whom shall I be afraid?" —Psalm 27:1 (The Clear Word)

In the fall of 1974, Cindy and I left Michigan and returned to the state of Maryland to continue my college education. Our first home in Maryland was living with Uncle Arthur and Aunt Pam Ambrose in Mitchellville, Maryland. We lived there for about four months, then we moved to a basement apartment on Willow avenue in Takoma Park, Maryland. One day we were pleasantly surprised by a visit from Cindy's grand-parents, Mr. & Mrs. Frank and Grace Bullock (affectionately referred to as Mom-Mom and Pop-Pop). They were the first members of Cindy's family to accept us into the Bullock family. They invited us to Chesapeake Camp Meeting and introduced us to many relatives and friends. One year after living at Willow avenue, we moved to a new apartment on Roanoke Avenue in Takoma Park.

On Sunday June 22nd, 1975, Cindy and I had a church wedding. We were married before the Justice of the Peace, at the court house in Berrien Springs, Michigan, on May 20th, 1974, but we wanted a marriage and wedding ceremony and reception. It was a wonderful event. Much planning and preparation went into making the event a success. We rented Riverside Baptist Church, located in Southwest Washington D.C. This was a picturesque site, near the banks of the Potomac river. Tuxedos for the wedding party were rented from Longs Formal Rentals and Sales. Flowers for the wedding were prepared by Takoma Park Florist. The wedding cake was specially prepared by Bernstein's Bakery. Decorations for the reception venue were acquired from Norris Party Bazaar. Our professional photographer was Mr. Joseph Davidson. A friend assisted Cindy in making her wedding dress. She purchased other accouterments from Bridal Services Boutique. We had three bridesmaids and three groomsmen. The bridesmaids were, Dr. Betty Martin, matron of honor, Beverly Snyder and Gail Brown. The groomsmen were Willie Davis, best man, Fritz Kreiger and John Monroe. Professor Paul Clark escorted Cindy down the aisle. Mrs. Mercedes Mundy was the organist for the wedding ceremony. The marriage ceremony was conducted by our pastor, Wayne Hicks, a Seventh-day Adventist minister. In addition to the aforementioned persons, some of the other guests in attendance were, Mr. & Mrs. Arthur & Pam Ambrose (uncle & wife), Ms. Claudia Ambrose (sister), Dr. John Ambrose (cousin), Dr. & Mrs. Lyndrey Niles, Ms. Judy Ambrose, Mrs. Paul Clark and daughter, Ms. Camille Mundy, Dr. Seth Lumbago and Ms. Mary Stroman. The wedding reception was held in a large adjacent room for the purpose of social gatherings.

After our wedding in 1975, for our honeymoon, we took a trip to the Caribbean-Trinidad and Saint Vincent. It was a beautiful October morning. We packed our bags and was ready to travel. We left our car with our church pastor and his family, and they drove us to Reagan National airport. This was an anxious event for my wife Cindy, because this was her first experience to fly in an airplane. She expressed concern and doubt whether the large Eastern Airlines aircraft would be able to make it up into the skies. I assured her that the pilot and co-pilot had safely taken the aircraft into the stratosphere many times before. About two hours in flight, dinner was served. We had a relatively smooth flight to Miami,

Florida. After about one hour and a half wait at the air terminal, we boarded a BWIA air line for the remainder of our trip.

Our plane made a stop on the island of Jamaica. While the plane was refueling, a mechanical problem was discovered. Everyone was requested to leave the plane. We were taken to a hotel to spend the night. This was about 10:00 p.m. At about 3:00 a.m. everyone was told to return to the airport because the mechanical problem was repaired. In the rush, many passengers became confused and angry. My wife and I included. We barely made it back to the airport, and continued our trip to Trinidad. When we landed at Piarco International Airport, my cousin Mona and her husband, John Thompson, were there to pick us up and took us to their home. In Trinidad we traveled, shopped, visited the beach, attended church, and Cindy was introduced to several of her new in-laws, including my dad. After spending a week in Trinidad, we flew to the island of St. Vincent. My mom and other family members, lived on another smaller island that is part of a group of small islands that comprised the country of St. Vincent. This island is called Union Island. With some difficulty and delay, we finally arrived at our destination by boat.

Our visit was a delightful and memorable occasion. My wife Cindy was introduced to my mother, my grandmother (maternal) and other family members. We ate fresh tropical fruits—papaya, golden apples, mangoes, bananas, oranges and grapes—every day. We visited the beach with family members and friends. When we returned to our apartment in Takoma Park, Maryland, we were very disappointed and shocked to discover that there was a fire in our apartment. Thank the Lord, everything was not destroyed, and most items were salvageable.

In December of 1975, I got a job as a phlebotomy technologist in the clinical laboratory at Washington Adventist Hospital. I experienced many joys and encountered several challenges there. During the course of my work, I had the privilege of meeting many different people from various walks of life. Our two children Eliot and Sean were born at Washington Adventist Hospital. My wife, Cindy, was born at this hospital. She also had a surgical procedure done at this facility. This was our family hospital. I worked for eight years as a full-time employee there. Several life-long friendships were formed during the time I worked at WAH.

In the spring of 1976, I registered for classes at Washington Adventist University and continued my undergraduate education. In July of 1977, Cindy complained of abdominal discomfort, frequent urination, and she also missed her monthly cycle. After doing a urine test for UGC, I discovered that she was pregnant with our first child. This news caused both excitement and some apprehension about the future. We were glad that our marriage had borne the blessings of a new life. We were also concerned as to how this event will change and affect our lives. The pregnancy went well and Cindy had a natural delivery. On April 5, 1978, Eliot Zephrine Edwards was born at Washington Adventist Hospital. He was delivered by our ob/gyn physician Dr. Neohr Steohr, Chief of the division of Obstetrics and Gynecology at the hospital. I was in the delivery (operating) room with my camera when Eliot came into the world. He was a beautiful baby with a very fair complexion. After Cindy spent a couple days in the hospital, we took our baby home. Cindy stayed home with Eliot, while I continued to work at Washington Adventist Hospital.

One day I received an emergency call. The call was from Cindy, my wife. "Zeph you've got to come home quickly, Eliot has stopped breathing and he seems to be turning blue!"

I listened as she spoke and I responded to her, "take him out of his crib, hold him in your left arm, and with two fingers of the right hand press down moderately on his mid chest (sternum) several times, check to make sure he's breathing. If he is, that's good. If not, then place your mouth over his nose and mouth and give him one full breath." I waited on the phone while she performed the procedure.

She responded, "he's breathing, he's breathing! After I pressed on his chest". This event occurred one other time when Eliot was a baby. This occurrence did have some adverse effect on Eliot's growth and development. His walking and talking functions developed later than usual. For about two years Eliot attended a developmental and rehabilitation program in Montgomery County that greatly assisted him with his personal challenges. After Eliot was born, we decided that Cindy should stay home from work and care for Eliot. This was a high stakes decision, but it was the right one. This situation placed added strain on my studies, work, and on me personally. In the course of trying to fulfill my obligations, goals, and commitments, I may have pushed myself a little harder than I should have. As a result, I experienced some severe motion sickness, nausea and fatigue. I did some blood tests, and the results were all satisfactory. This was good news, but the same symptoms continued to interrupt my daily routine. I eventually went to the emergency room! My eyes and ears were checked and I was given a prescription for some Antivert. This medication was for inner ear imbalance. I consulted with a trusted physician and he said that this condition appears to be viral rather than organic in nature.

That same year, 1979, the Lord protected and delivered Cindy from a potentially dangerous automobile accident. She usually travelled everywhere with baby Eliot in the car with her, however, on this particular day, I was home, therefore she decided to leave Eliot with me. While she was driving, the brakes on the Dodge Charger gave way. She ran through a red light and hit a parked truck. She struck her forehead and sustained a bump. That was the extent of her injury! We were very glad that Eliot was not with her in the car at that time. Praise the Lord for his goodness!

Eliot had some difficulty keeping up with his studies when we placed him in a regular school program in elementary and high school. He did receive assistance from special education teachers. He finished school in the tenth grade and received a high school certificate. He later graduated from a six-month training program in food technology and held a full-time position in the field.

My college experience was difficult, intense, and delightful. Part of my difficulty was not mastering the art of how to study properly. This process got better as I advanced through my college years. The experience was intense because I usually had a full schedule—wife, two small children, classes, study, work, president of the psychology club, and church obligations. I also enjoyed meeting many different students from several countries—England, Russia, Spain, Japan, Germany, Latin America, Canada as well from different parts of the United States. I started my college education at Prince George's Community College in Largo, Maryland. During my sophomore year, I transferred to Andrews University in Berrien Springs, Michigan. I then transferred to Washington Adventist University in Takoma Park, Maryland where I graduated with a BA degree in psychology, with a minor in religion. I took additional college courses at three other colleges in Maryland. I attended graduate school at Liberty University in Lynchburg, Virginia, for counseling psychology, and attended medical school—Universidad Central del Este, School of Medicine in San Pedro de Macoris—Dominican Republic. During my senior year as a student at Washington Adventist University, I was elected as president of the psychology club. This was truly a special honor. This task involved presiding and coordinating the committees and activities of the psychology club. My obligations and efforts were also to broaden an understanding of the field of psychology, and the role of the professional psychologist. Owing to my busy schedule, this was the only extra-curricular activity I allowed myself. I further sought to foster an interchange of ideas among psychology majors at the university.

On April 26th, 1980 I finally achieved, with the help of our Almighty Father, the goal of graduating from college with a bachelor's degree in psychology and a minor in religion. This was truly an historic milestone in my life's journey. During the graduation weekend, Cindy's mom, Natalie Bullock, came to Takoma Park, Maryland, from Berrien Springs, Michigan to celebrate this important occasion with us.

For the Christmas of 1980, we took the opportunity and traveled north to Berrien Springs, Michigan to spend this special time with Cindy's folks. This was a most joyous time and delightful experience. I visited several of Cindy's family members that I had not met before. To my surprise, I was well received by all. This trip afforded me a deeper insight into the nature and characteristics of her family background. I learned about her family experience in Port Deposit, Maryland, before her family moved to Michigan for work. For the very first time I rode on a snowmobile. I enjoyed snowmobiles rides with Cindy's sister, Sue, and her husband Perry Nelson. We enjoyed our visits and stayed with Sue and Perry Nelson and their daughter, April. We also had wonderful meal times and get-togethers with other members of the family.

In June of 1980 we moved from Roanoke Avenue in Takoma Park to Nob Hill apartments on Piney Branch road in Silver Springs, Maryland. My wife Cindy became pregnant with our second child in January 1981. Sean was born at Washington Adventist hospital in Takoma Park, Maryland on September 24th, 1981. Like our first son Eliot, his delivery was natural and without incident. He was a beautiful and chubby baby. I continued working as a phlebotomy technologist in the clinical laboratory at Washington Adventist Hospital. My job involved drawing blood specimens from patients on the various wards of the hospital. I preformed clinical assays on patients and assisted student workers and new employees in the orientation process. At the end of five (5) years of service as a full-time employee, I received a 5 year award pin and a letter of commendation at a special banquet for all such employees. I worked at several different hospitals in the Washington Metropolitan area as a phlebotomist or as a clinical laboratory technician. Some of the places I worked were, Greater Southeast Community Hospital in Washington D.C., Suburban Hospital in

Bethesda, Maryland, Providence Hospital in Washington D.C., Children's Hospital National Medical Center in Washington D.C., and Lee Memorial Hospital in Dowagiac, Michigan. As a clinical laboratory technician I worked in different sections of the laboratory. I worked in hematology, urinalysis, blood bank (immunohematology), and chemistry.

In June of 1982, we received a letter from Uncle John and Aunt Pat (Cindy's side of the family) inviting us to a Bullock's family reunion in Owensboro, Kentucky. Our first and immediate reaction was a negative response. Owing to past reactions of family members to our marriage, we felt that it may be unwise to attend such a gathering. After a couple weeks elapsed, we received a telephone call from Aunt Pat, asking about our plans concerning attending the reunion. We told her that owing to financial constraints, we could not afford to make the trip. This was the truth. To our great surprise, they sent us the money for the trip. They said that they really wanted us to come, and would really appreciate if we would make the effort to be there. We changed our minds and decided to attend the family reunion. This was a most unforgettable experience! Our impression was that there was a genuine attempt to make us feel welcome and a part of the family.

Saturday, July 3, 1982, started with a wonderful breakfast. The family gathered and sang songs—mainly religious songs. Saturday is the weekly day of worship for Seventh-day Adventist. After the singing was over, we had a time of self-identification and testimony. Different family members told how they met their spouses, girlfriends or boyfriends, how long they've been together and other aspects of their lives. After lunch, the family gathering visited Lincoln State Park, and had a wonderful time there. Independence Day, Sunday July 4th, was also a delightful day of various games, quiet time, family closeness, and of course the big event that capped off the entire day—the fireworks extravaganza. The bus trip to The Grand Ole Opry in Tennessee was another delightful event. This opportunity provided more time for closeness and sharing. My most enjoyable events at Opryland were observing the grizzly bears and participating in the water rafting. Our journey back home to Maryland was long and tedious. We were detoured three times, but we finally made it home safely. We thanked the Lord for a successful trip.

Later in July, 1982 I attended my brother Althus' wedding in Toronto, Canada. This was another wonderful time spent with many family members (Zeph's side of the family) and friends. Work obligations and other commitments did not permit Cindy and our children to accompany me to Canada. I stayed at my uncle Colis' home, with his wife and family. This was a special time for at least three reasons. First, it was my brother's wedding and I wanted to be there; secondly, some years have passed, since I'd visited with my family members and friends; and thirdly, my family and I had planned to leave the United States for the Dominican Republic in the next year, 1983, in order to attend medical school. I did not know when I would have the opportunity to visit with my family members again! Denise, the bride-to-be, was sitting in the living room with other wedding guests. In the course of conversation Denise's aunt, Modecene, extended an invitation to me and my family to visit England. They travelled from England, for the purpose of attending the wedding. I gladly accepted the invitation to visit them in England, at some future date.

Chapter 4
Medical School in the Dominican Republic

"When you walk through waters, I will be with you. When you pass through swollen rivers, they will not flow over you. When you walk through fire, you will not be burned, neither will the flames harm you."—Isaiah 43:2 (The Clear Word)

After working eight years as a full-time employee in the clinical laboratory at Washington Adventist Hospital, I decided to apply to medical school. I applied to several medical schools, inside and outside the United States. I received letters from some schools, stating that I was on a waiting list. I was accepted by two medical schools. I decided to attend UCE—Universidad Central del Este Escuela de Medicina (Central Eastern University School of Medicine) located in the city of San Pedro (Saint Peter) in the Dominican Republic. My family and I sold most of our belongings. I left three boxes of my college books with friends.

There was a reception at my job at Washington Adventist hospital and a bon voyage party at the church for my family and me. The two occasions were truly impressive and genuinely touching. We received gifts and postcards filled with the names of dear friends and well-wishers.

After Cindy and I resigned our jobs, we flew to Tampa, Florida, where Cindy's grandparents were living at the time. I left Cindy and our two boys in Tampa, and continued on to the Dominican Republic. After finding an apartment, I registered for my classes. About a month after I arrived, my family joined me in San

Pedro (St. Peter's city), Dominican Republic. The city is a relatively small place, located about 70 miles east of Santo Domingo, the capital city of the Dominican Republic. The outskirts of the City were pastoral and country-like. Great areas were occupied by sugar cane and corn field. I attended classes while Cindy and the boys stayed at home. The experience of living and going to school, with a family, in a foreign country, have been a very difficult and challenging one. There were the concerns of a different language, culture, foods, and customs. For the most part, the Dominican people are a warm, affable and friendly people. My family and I appreciated this warmth and friendship. Most of the Americans did as well.

    The lectures for my classes were in Spanish, so were the textbooks, laboratories, exams, and everything else. This involved a lot of extra studying. I usually studied the English (American) medical textbooks for a good grasp and understanding of the lesson content, and then studied the Spanish text. Many American and Canadian students joined our Spanish counterparts and studied in small groups. This approach greatly augmented the learning process. Most week-ends were spent with my family, attending church and visiting many parts of the Dominican Republic, and other families. Most Dominicans are kind and hospitable to visitors and foreigners when they're treated with dignity, respect, and friendliness. Many dress neatly and nicely and they appreciate clean surroundings. My observations were that there were no sizable middle class. There were the extremely rich people and the extremely poor people. However, many of the poor people seemed to be happy and content, in spite of their poverty.

    Catholicism is the prevalent faith for most Dominicans. As a result, there were statues and obelisks in people's homes. People believed in saints to petition the divine, in their behalf. There was also the concept that human beings were inadequate (unworthy) to come to God on their own accord, without an intermediary. People depended on forms, religious ceremonies, and traditions, rather than on a personal and serious commitment to God, and the call of the Christian life. There is a strong belief in the notion that one's life was controlled by predestined fate and destiny; therefore there were uncontrollable forces that determined a person future and destiny, regardless of one's personal choices. As a result, the concept and the sense of personal responsibility and accountability are qualities that are seriously lacking. The Dominican Republic has many natural resources—gold, oil, copra, sugar, caco, coffee—but it is not being aggressively developed for the benefit of all the people. While I was a medical student, there were no dole or welfare systems to help poor people. An excellent feature of Dominican life is the diverse and cosmopolitan makeup of its people. Its population is made up of Chinese, Africans, Indians, Arabs, Jews, Europeans, Cubans, Puerto-Ricans, and many others.

Class divisions are more evident than ethnic, racial, or cultural distinctions. In this society, the man (male) is definitely the superior of the species. The concept of machismo is very present in the culture.

My family and I had wonderful times when we lived in the Dominican Republic. However, this period of time was a very difficult and stressful time for my wife. She experienced severe culture shock, owing to the differences in the language, the food, the environment, and the customs of the Latin (Spanish) society. After much contemplation and discussion she decided to return to her parents in Michigan in the U.S., until I finished the school term. Shortly after my wife returned to the United States, a very unfortunate situation developed in the Dominican Republic.

Owing to an economic shortfall of agricultural products, the Dominican government raised food prices throughout the country. Almost immediately food riots broke out in several cities. The system of democracy that existed in the Dominican Republic at that time was symbolized by a small "D". The government was definitely not as tolerant as the system that existed in the United States. A state of emergency was instituted. Army units were stationed throughout the country to suppress the riots. The airports were shut down! No one was allowed to leave the country! Mobs looted stores, shops, and other businesses in different parts of the country! Many looters were shot dead on the spot! International news organizations covered the situation. The medical school closed down and students, faculty, and staff were told to stay in their homes. By this time my wife and our two kids had safely arrived at her parent's home in Berrien Springs, Michigan. They saw the riots, violence, and shootings on television. My wife called, and she was able to get through to me! She said, "Mom and Dad and everyone here at home, saw what was happening in the Dominican Republic. Are you in a safe place, are you o.k.?"

I replied, "I'm here in my apartment. Everyone was asked to stay in their homes, until it was safe to go outside! How are you and our kids doing?"

She replied, "the kids and I are doing well, but we miss you terribly. What are your future plans? How long do you plan to stay there? Do you plan to join us anytime soon?"

I responded, "I plan to finish out the school term, then I will come to Michigan." We spoke about twenty to thirty minutes concerning several family matters. She finally told me to take care and she would keep me in her thoughts and prayers. This conversation was followed up with letters from both of us. This period of time in my life was one of deep reflection and soul searching. I considered and thought of the meaning and nature of genuine love, the moral obligations of the marriage covenant, and the solemn responsibilities of a family. The deep convictions of my Christian faith sustained me during this experience. I learned lessons and drew comfort from the example of the prophet Hosea and his wife Gomer, the waiting father (story of the prodigal son), and the story of the good Samaritan. In each of these stories the guilty parties did not receive what they deserved, but what they needed. They deserved punishment and death, but instead they were given forgiveness, compassion and mercy. Only God can give human being the ability to offer forgiveness, compassion and kindness even though one was wronged. At the end of the school term, I returned to my family in Berrien Springs, Michigan. Even though I did not fulfill my dream of becoming a medical doctor, the ensuing years have shown me that, even though this was a very hard decision, it was the right decision.

After I settled down with my family, I began the process of seeking employment. For a period of nine months I unsuccessfully looked for work in the states of Michigan and Ohio. In the winter of 1984, during a job fair at Andrews University in Berrien Springs, Michigan, I was recruited as a literature sales representative (colporteur) by the Pennsylvania Conference of Seventh-day Adventist. My area of assignment was Pittsburg, Pennsylvania. The senior sales representative for that area was Mr. Bill Haper. He assisted me in finding a place to live temporarily, in Greenburg, PA. After training with him for one month, I found a more permanent place to stay in Oakland, PA., a town on the outskirts of Pittsburg. After finding this apartment for rent, I brought my family from Michigan to Oakland, PA. This was a time of challenges and excitement. The salary I earned for my work as a sales representative was based on commission, which depended on my volume of sales. This necessitated me spending many hours in the field, away from my family. Sometimes, I did take Cindy and our two boys with me. The work was fascinating and instructive. It entailed a good knowledge of the products I was selling, the ability to quickly form deep human relationships, and demonstrate to clients that the product will meet and satisfy their needs.

The training that I received at the Columbia Union Conference of Seventh-day Adventist, in Columbia, MD, helped me to master the art of memorization and reading books and other literature upside down. I learned many techniques in ascertaining people's interest and then demonstrating to them that the health and spiritual books that I was selling will meet their deepest physical, mental and spiritual needs. Some of the books that I sold were namely: *Health and Happiness, The Desire of Ages, The Bible Stories, The Great Controversy,* "Vibrant Life," "Listen," and "Winner" magazines, and also other *Conflict of the Ages* books. I was fortunate to have the opportunity to be trained in the field by excellent sales professionals like Mrs. Sandy Dancek and Bill Haper. I experienced many deep and rich spiritual events during the eight months that I worked as a full-time colporteur for the Pennsylvania Conference of SDA. My work was principally in the city of Pittsburg and the surrounding vicinity—Monroeville, McKeesport, and Greensburg. Since I played a wind harp (harmonica), I was asked to perform special music for several churches. I was also asked to preach the sermon on a few occasions.

One of my most memorable and thrilling experiences, was my encounter with a client by the name of Mrs. Annie Brown. At the time I met Annie, she was living in the city of Pittsburg, PA, and was going through a separation and divorce from her husband. He moved out of their home and was living with a younger woman. Annie was very distraught and broken up about this situation. She asked me, "Why would my husband do something like this, after we've been married for so many years?"

I replied, "I do not have an answer Annie." She went on to explain to me in some detail, many difficulties and trials that they experienced throughout their marriage. She broke down and cried several times as she told me her story. Even though she did not have the money to purchase the health and religious books and products that I was selling, the visits and telephone conversations were therapeutic sessions.

After working as a full-time colporteur for eight (8) months, my family and I moved to the capital, Harrisburg, PA. We lived in a suburban town called Colonial Park, about three miles outside the city of Harrisburg. Our two boys, Eliot and Sean, were getting older, and we needed a larger financial income to meet the increasing demands of our family. In January 1986, I started working in the clinical laboratory at Poly-clinic Hospital in Harrisburg as a phlebotomy technologist. My job entailed drawing blood samples for various tests from patients throughout the hospital. I did this on a part time basis for four months. In June, 1986, I got a better paying job at Sera Tec, Biologicals, even though this was also part time employment. This facility was also in Harrisburg. The work consisted of drawing blood from qualified clients (the public) who were paid a fee for a bag of their blood. This company supplied blood banks and hospitals with blood products for the purpose of transfusions, surgeries, and other medical uses. I worked at this facility for seven months. In addition to being a clinical laboratory technician I am also a certified phlebotomy technologist.

The Lord opened the way, and I was fortunate to pass a state qualifying examination. As a result I received a full scholarship that enabled me to take a nursing (LPN) course for twelve months. I attended the Harrisburg Steelton Highspire School of Nursing. The program started in September 1986 and ended in August 1987. The nursing program was later moved to the Harrisburg Area Community College (HACC). This was a very demanding and challenging course of study. The fact that I was a college graduate, greatly contributed to my success. A quarter of the students who started the course dropped out for different reasons.

The following experience marked a very important juncture while I was a student in the nursing program. I made excellent grades in the academic areas of the nursing programs. However, I had some difficulty with the clinical aspect of the program. One day I was called into the program director, Ms. Carlyn Forlizzli's, office and was told that I was being discharged from the nursing program. I went into a state of shock, after I was given this news! I told Ms. Forlizzli that I had good grades in all other aspects of the program, and I requested a chance to improve my performance in the clinical area in which I was deficient. Her mind was made up, and therefore she did not grant my request. My feelings of loss and disappointment was inexpressible. I left her office in a daze,

My Journey of Discovery

collected my belongings, and made my way downstairs. As I was about to exit the building, I thought to myself that I should stop at the school administrator's office and present my case for a hearing one more time. This was one of the most pleasant and dramatic surprises of my life! All of the teachers and most of the students in the school of nursing were Caucasian. I entered the administrator's office, and asked to see the principal about an urgent matter. A slim and tall African-American woman came out to meet me. I could not believe my eyes! I collected myself and breathed a sigh of relief! "Hello, Mr. Edwards, how may I help you?"

"Hello Ms. Juainta Moore. I'm hopeful that you can help me with my situation. I've been a student in the nursing program for the last eight months. I've passed my exams and excelled in all areas of the program, except a clinical component of the course. I have been improving, however, Ms. Forlizzli was not satisfied with my progress. As a consequence, she dismissed me from the nursing program twenty-five minutes ago. I would like to be given the opportunity to finish the program." To my surprise, Ms. Moore became quite perturbed and asked me to accompany her to Ms. Forlizzli's office—I was not prepared for what happened next! We ascended the staircase to the floor above, where the nursing school was located. She knocked on Ms. Forlizzli's office door, and we entered her office together.

"Hi Carlyn, Mr. Edwards was just in my office. He told me that you dismissed him from the nursing program, even though he passed all areas of the course, but he was having some difficulties with the clinical aspects of the program. I gave you extra money in the budget for cases such as Mr. Edwards, and I want to have Mr. Edwards reinstated into the program."

Ms. Forlizzi replied, "I will reinstate Mr. Edwards in the program and work with him to strengthen and improve his clinical nursing skills." I thanked Ms. Carlyn Forlizzi and Ms. Juainta Moore, but my deepest and most profound gratitude and thanks were given to my Lord and Savior Jesus Christ. I worked harder, completed the course of study, and graduated from the nursing program in August 1987. This experience left a lasting impression on my mind and heart.

After graduating from the nursing program, I worked in several part time nursing positions. I took the civil service exams in the state of Pennsylvania, and eventually got a job with the U.S. government, working as a nurse at the Veterans Hospital Center in Lebanon, Pennsylvania. After more than one attempt, I succeeded in passing the national board exam in nursing, and received my nursing license in 1989. Working as a nurse at the Veteran's Administration Medical Center was an experience that I shall always remember. I acquired a real appreciation for the military men and women who served our country and bore the wounds and lingering scars of war. I shall not soon forget two special patients that were assigned to me as I worked on the medical-surgical unit at the hospital. These two patients were soldiers in the U.S. Army. They both had acquired immune deficiency syndrome (AIDS). The disease was ravishing their bodies! This was one of the two most challenging experiences I had as a nurse when I worked at the VA hospital. I had a particularly difficult time owing to the cognitive dissonance I experiences regarding AIDS. I had a less difficult time caring for my patient who contracted AIDS as a result of drug addiction than the Army Colonel who got the disease as a result of his lifestyle as a homosexual man. I resolved my dilemma when I considered that these two soldiers deserved my care and attention, because they both gave themselves in service to our country. I therefore did put aside my Christian morality and rendered the professional and caring services that they needed and deserved.

In the spring of 1990, I started doing a master's degree program in counseling psychology at Liberty University. Another very challenging experience occurred when I was assigned to the Alzheimer's unit. I had to learn the skills of patience and tolerance, which I did not realize I had the ability to develop. The disease of

Alzheimer's seems to defy all reason, logic, and understanding regarding its impact on patients and how it manifests itself. Even though I took care of the same patients each day (some more than others) some would respond as if I'd never taken care of them. They had very little memory or recollection of the experience. Many activities of daily living, dressing a wound, and administering medications were a difficult chore. My most satisfying nursing experience was when I worked on the medical-surgical and psychiatric units. As an African-American and a male nurse, I was surprised to learn and experience the gender and racial bias that existed in the nursing profession in general and in Lebanon, Pennsylvania in particular. After living in Pennsylvania for five years, my wife and I returned to our home state of Maryland to settle down and raise our family.

Chapter 5

From Pennsylvania back To Maryland

"If you start turning to the right or to the left you will hear a still, small voice saying, Over here is the way; walk in it." — Isaiah 30:21 (The Clear Word)

After deciding to return to our home state of Maryland to live and settle down, we made application seeking employment in Maryland. I finally found a job as an addiction nurse at Mountain Manor Treatment Center in Emmitsburg, Maryland. I was really excited about this position, because I've always enjoyed working in the field of addictionology. The work was challenging, exciting, and rewarding. In the field of addiction one is exposed to the full range of human nature and experience. The program at the treatment center was a 28 day program. A patient or resident had to be mandated by a given authority, such as one's employer or the courts, to be eligible for admission into the program. If a resident failed to comply with the rules and regulation of the program, that person would most likely lose his/her job or would be sent to jail, as the case may be. I will always remember this particular patient (resident). I will call her Mary. She was mandated to the treatment program by the courts with a diagnosis of drug and sexual addiction. Each client's diagnosis was confidential, unless the client chose to divulge the reason for the admission into the program. Mary chose to share her diagnosis with a few clients that she thought that she could trust. In a short period of time, just about everyone knew her diagnosis, and that she also had AIDS. Mary had blonde hair, with medium height (5'8") and medium built (mesomorph), and she was moderately attractive. She had her young son in the program with her (he could have been 9 or 10 years old). Even though the men in program knew that it was against the rules, and that Mary had HIV, they still propositioned her for sex. I was astounded and disturbed by this development. I came to learn and understand the powerful nature of addiction. Against the entreaties and counsel of many staff members and clients in the program, Mary left the program one morning about 2:00 a.m., and hitch-hiked about 30 miles to Washington DC to get cocaine from her dealer. She was shaking and had to get a fix!

The daily commute from Harrisburg, PA to Emmitsburg, MD was fifty (50) miles one way. We decided to look for housing in the city of Frederic, MD which was just south of the town of Emmitsburg. One day, after house hunting, we decided to return home to Pennsylvania but by a different way than when we had come to Maryland. We came down on highway 15 and decided to return home on interstate 83. We took highway 140, and traveled from west to east. This highway connects interstate 15 to interstate 83. After travelling for about 30 minutes, we came through a city called Westminster. We stopped at a laundromat and brought some refreshments. While we were in the facility we met a lady. This was a Sunday. She was in her mid-twenties. She had finished washing her clothes and wanted a ride home. She was restricted from driving, owing to a medical condition. She requested of me, "Sir, can you give me a ride to my house, I don't have my own transportation?"

I responded, "lady my family and I are just passing through this city, we've never been here before and we really don't know anything about this place. We're planning to relocate to Maryland, and we just came from Frederick, where we were trying to find housing and a school for our kids."

Debbie introduced herself to us. "I can show you where I live" she continued. After a little thought and some conversation, we decided to take her home. She said, "if you're looking for a church school for your two boys, we have one here in Westminster." We discovered that Debbie was a Seventh-day Adventist like we are. Together, we visited Crest Lane S.D.A. Elementary School. We met Mrs. Charlotte Becker, the principal, and her husband. We made the move from Colonial Park, a suburb of Harrisburg, PA, to the city of Westminster, M (about 40 to 50 miles north of Washington D.C.) in the year 1990. If this experience did not happen to me, I would have a difficult time believing it occurred, the way it did. The same day that we met Debbie Wantz at the laundromat, she directed us to Crest Lane SDA elementary school. We met and spoke with Mrs. Charlotte Becker, the school's principal. We tentatively, enrolled Eliot and Sean in Crest Lane School, and with Debbie's assistance, was able to make definite plans of securing an apartment for our family in the same building in which she was living. We eventually got the apartment directly above Debbie and Steve Wantz's apartment. As we drove back home to Pennsylvania that day, we knew beyond the shadow of a doubt that the hand of the Lord had guided our every action that day.

    We moved to 37 Sullivan Avenue in Westminster, Maryland, and lived there for three years, while we looked for a home to purchase. Cindy got a job with Westminster Nursing and Rehabilitation Center. This facility was part of the same parent company—Beverly Enterprise Inc.—that she worked for in Pennsylvania. This meant that her employment was treated as a transfer, with all the benefits and advantages, instead of starting over as a new employee. This was truly a blessing! I got a new job as a Maryland State employee, at Spring Grove Hospital Center as a nurse. This was a time of enormous challenge and stress. Spring Grove hospital was a mental health facility. This was a very different kind of nursing than medical-surgical nursing. I had to quickly acquaint myself with a thorough knowledge of psychotropic medications and therapies. The orientation and education regimen was long and intense. My undergraduate and graduate education in psychology was of immense value in helping me to navigate through this challenging experience.

The following case history is an example of the kind of patients I cared for at Spring Grove Hospital Center. I will call this patient Henry Wells. I met and conferenced with Mr. Henry Wells concerning his presenting diagnosis. He became evasive and denied being responsible for any of the issues that he was having problems with. He stated "I didn't do any of these things that I was accused of." The patient continued eye contact with staff and was obviously uncomfortable discussing his problems. Henry indicated that he understood that his behaviors were socially unacceptable. I met with Henry twice weekly to discuss his feelings and review this patient's personal hygiene. Owing to a mismatch in his clothing and disheveled appearance, this patient had to be observed closely to insure proper grooming. Mr. Wells had been educated about his personal hygiene, and using the bathroom to wash himself at regular intervals. Henry's appearance would be checked regularly after he would leave his ward to go outside. This patient was praised for his improvement in judgement. He stated that he always washed his hands and put on underwear, however, staff sometimes had to remind him of these matters. Sometimes this patient took a daily bath in order to maintain his personal hygiene. All relevant staff members were required to help him to maintain his personal hygiene, and use the bathroom regularly. When Mr. Wells was ready for discharge, the social worker would investigate supervised community housing. All of Henry's medical problems would be cared for by the somatic physician and he would be made aware of any physical complaints he might have. This patient's father mentioned an interest in his program. He visited and often took him home with him on weekends when his behavior was appropriate. Henry's ITP (Individual treatment plan) would be maintained and staff would continue to give support and educate this patient in appropriate maters and give positive feedback as necessary.

In response to my application for a new job with the State of Maryland, I received a reply on October 26, 1992, indicating that I had been selected for a nursing position at Rosewood Center. This medical state facility catered mostly to patients and clients who had mild, moderate, and profound mental and physical disability. Without a doubt this was the most difficult and challenging job I'd undertaken in my entire working career. After the period of orientation was completed, I felt so overwhelmed and intimidated that I was sure that I would resign the job. I'm not sure what motivated me to return the next day. However, I believed that it was my need and obligation to support my family. I decided to take one step at a time and live one day at a time. I also earnestly sought for divine guidance and courage to face this challenging experience. As time passed, I surprisingly became more and more acclimated to the patients and my nursing duties. I had never encountered nor seen more profound deformity in human beings as I saw at Rosewood Center. I have had conversations with staff who believed that these patients were not created by God, and therefore treated them with disdain and cruelty. As a result, I experienced a great deal of cognitive and moral dissonance, regarding the way in which several staff members treated patients and clients in the facility. My Christian faith also made me an automatic target for certain staff members. My supervisor, Mr. Frank, was a homosexual, and a co-worker, Ms. Lillian L., was a lesbian. They had a natural disdain for Christians and the Christian faith. I did my best to be kind, courteous, and respectful to them as fellow workers. However, their attitude and conduct towards me was quite unprofessional at times.

The following incidences were examples of mischievous and malicious actions. I was asked to work overtime on Monday in the morning on April 5, 1993. I was assigned to Cook and John's cottages. The supervisor for Paca unit, Mr. Frank S., also worked in Cook cottage on Monday, April 5, 1993. At about 10:00 a.m., I went out and had a snack brunch. On my return to John's cottage, I called Mr. S. and let him know I had returned. There was work to be done in John's cottage, so I stayed there and carried on with my duties. At about 1:00 p.m. Mr. S. called me in his office in John's cottage and asked how I was doing. I told him that two clients were having vomiting problems and that I was in the process of sending one of them to the clinic as requested by the doctor. I gave him reports on some other patients, and he told me that he would present the report when the two shifts met to give report on the clients at two o'clock p.m. He then asked me if I needed any help. I told him that I could manage the situation on my own. Mr. Frank S. never told me that, on Monday, April 5, 1993, while I was in John's cottage, Dr. O'Campo wrote orders on two clients—Clarence L. and Anthony G. He also did not post the physician orders. Yellow stickers that were supposed to be placed on the client's charts, to identify them, were not on the charts. Consequently, I did not know about the physician orders and I did not post and carry out the orders. The nurse, R.W., who worked the 11-7 shift also did not post the orders, because the yellow dots were not on the two clients' charts in question. I was off duty the following Tuesday.

  When I returned to work on Wednesday, Mr. Frank S. had a conference with me. During the conference, I learned from him, that he knew that Dr. O'Campo had written those orders. However, Mr. S. never mentioned anything to me about those doctor's orders. As a result of this conference, Mr. Frank S. wrote me a letter of reprimand. I refused to sign the letter, and made an appointment to have a conference with the director of nursing. After the matter was investigated, Mr. Frank S. was ordered to rescind the letter of reprimand. Thank the Lord for His protection in this situation.

  The following incident that transpired on Thursday, October 21, 1993 was in reference to influenza vaccine Trivalent A and B, 0.5ml Im. that were ordered by the physician to be administered to three different clients in Cook's cottage. The supervisor for Paca unit, Mr. Frank S., RN, directed in the nursing report that vaccines be given to the afore-mentioned clients. No consent forms accompanied the vaccines. Ms. Buelah, RN, and I searched for the consent forms everywhere in the medication rooms in Cook's cottage, but did not find them. The matter was told to Ms. Delores P., RN, The nursing supervisor on duty that evening. Mr. Frank S., RN, was fully aware of the negative consequences, had I given the vaccines to those clients without prior consent. That same day, 10/21/93, Mr. S. was listening to the nursing report at the change of shifts and heard Ms. Evelyn W., RN, Primary Care Coordinator, as she spoke in detail and at length about the consent forms and that they must be signed before the vaccines can be given. Mr. Frank S. had the consent forms in his possessions at that very time, but said nothing to me or anyone else, concerning the vaccines that were in Cook's cottage, that he directed ought to be administered by me. He deliberately withheld the consent forms in order to bring about an unfortunate situation. I later understood from my supervisor, Ms. Virginia G., RN, that Mr. Frank S. had placed the consent forms in his brief case and took them home with him. The next day, 10/22/93, he directed that three clients and an additional client be given the vaccines on my shift. When he was confronted about the situation, he produced the consent forms and the vaccines were administered in the proper manner. I thanked the Lord for his tender mercies in this situation.

    The following three episodes were designed to implicate me in negligent and unprofessional conduct by Ms. Lillian L., LPN. On Monday 9th, May 1994, at the beginning of the 2:00–10:30 p.m. shift in Cook's cottage, the following medications (that were supposed to have been dispensed and I did give) were found in a pill cup in a patient cassette: 6 red pills, 3 Serentil 10 mg and 3 Serentil 50mg, opened in a medication cup. These medications were to be given at bedtime. I notified the supervisor on duty. She came and saw the medications in the cup. Ms. Richards, RN, who worked the 2:00-10:30 p.m. shift in Cook's cottage on Friday 6th May, 1994, said that she did not see any pills in a cup in the patient's (in question) medication drawer in Cook's cottage. The medications were placed in the patient's cassette by Ms. Lillian L., LPN, who worked Saturday 7th and Sunday 8th May, 1994. On Monday 21st March, 1994, on the 2:00-10:30 p.m. shift in Cook's cottage, one Dilantin 100 mg tablet was left opened in a pill cup in a patient's medication drawer. Ms. Virginia G., RN, supervisor on duty, was notified. She came and saw the pill in the patient's cassette. Ms. Lillian L., LPN, worked on the day shift on the 21st of March 1994, and left that pill in the patient's cup. On Monday 17th January, 1994, on the 2:00-10:30 p.m. shift in Cook's cottage, the p.m. medications for the patient G.O. were left in a pill cup in his medication drawer. Ms. Lillian L., LPN, worked the previous shift, 7:00 a.m.–3:00 p.m., and on Saturday 15th and Sunday 16th of January, 1994, and placed those pills in the patient's medication drawer, in order to maliciously implicate me. The Lord protected me from the dire consequences in these situations!

In spite of the many difficult and challenging experiences as an employee at Rosewood Center, there were enjoyable and satisfying events as well. After the extension of my probationary period, I was pleased to have achieved permanent status as a Maryland State employee. On February 10th, 1994, I received a letter of recommendation from the director of the department of nursing for reporting to work during a snow emergency. As a result of being a member of the "Nurses Week" committee, I was instrumental in the planning and execution of a successful program for "Nurses Week" celebrations. Owing to the deep and challenging situations I experienced at Rosewood Center, I truly acquired the ability to integrate and bring my theoretical and practical knowledge of nursing together, and function as an effective and caring professional. I gained knowledge into human nature, sickness, disease, and the satisfaction that my nursing and professional skills made a critical difference in the lives of the clients who were committed to my charge and care.

In July 1992, I traveled to Toronto, Canada to attend my nephew's wedding. Althus was married to Denise. She was married before and had one child from her previous marriage. She had two aunts and a cousin who traveled from England in order to attend the wedding in Canada. The day before the wedding, several of the wedding guests sat in the living room of my Uncle Colis' home, discussing different topics. I became involved in a conservation with some of Denise relatives, Ms. Totmiller, Ms. Docene, and Ms. Doreen, from England, who were invited to the wedding. I indicated that it would be wonderful if I had the opportunity to visit England someday. Ms. Totmiller replied, "you and your family are welcome to visit England and stay at our home." I thought she was kidding!

I said excitedly, "are you serious"?

She said "of course, I'll be delighted to have you and your family visit us in England!"

I responded, "I accept your offer and we will make preparations to visit next year, 1993." On the morning of Tuesday, 24th August, 1993, my family and I, flew out of Baltimore Thurgood Marshall International Airport. After travelling for about twelve hours, we landed at Gatwick International airport in England. We were met at the airport by Ms. Totmiller. We were all exhausted from travelling, but we were happy and excited to have arrived safely in England. On Wednesday, August 25th, we toured London and visited Newbold College in Binfield. We took the train South to London, and then took a double-decker bus, west to Binfield. The city of Binfield is a quaint and small college town with beautiful Victorian houses. We visited Newbold College and thoroughly enjoyed its scenic and beautiful campus. We spoke to some of the students. The student body was very diverse and represented many different countries of the world. It was getting late in the day, and we decided to make our way back to London, in order to catch the train back to High Wycombe, the town where we were staying.

A funny event transpired while we were waiting for the bus to arrive, to take us to London. We were waiting for our bus on the right-hand side of the road. We had temporarily forgotten that we were in England, where they drove on the left-hand side of the road. After waiting for some time, a lady approached us—she apparently was watching us from her house. She asked us where we were going. I replied "We're waiting for the bus to take us to London, where we can get a train to take us to High Wycombe."

She replied, "You'll never get a bus to take you to London, if you wait on this side of the road! You must wait on the left-hand side of the road." Realizing that we were Americans, she proceeded to ask us a lot of questions about the United States. "Does everyone in America own guns?" I told her that the second amendment to the U.S. constitution allows American citizens to own guns. She seemed quite surprised about that fact. She continued, "Have you visited big cities like Los Angeles?"

I responded, "I've visited New York City, Philadelphia, Detroit and Chicago, but not Los Angeles."

Her questions kept coming. "I've seen very tall buildings, and wide streets on television, are they really like that?"

I said, "yes, that's the way they are." After talking for a while, our bus came and we made our way to London. We caught a train to the city of High Wycombe and retired from a long day.

On Thursday 26th August 1993, we returned to London by train. We took a tour bus. This was a double-decker bus, with the top completely opened. The bus drove to Buckingham Palace, the official residence of the British royal family, the Tower of London, Piccadilly Circus, Trafalgar Square, and other sites. We did some sightseeing in London and returned home that night. The next day, Friday 27th August, we decided to spend the day shopping and sightseeing in the city of High Wycombe, instead of travelling to

London. During that day, we exited a store in which we were shopping. As Cindy, my wife, stepped off the curb, a car swung around the corner, and would have killed her on the spot! We believe that an angel of the Lord protected her from sudden death! The next day, Saturday 28th, August we attended church and enjoyed a full and wonderful day. I played my harp (harmonica) for special music. We were invited out to dinner and enjoyed delicious food and wonderful fellowship. Our host drove us to several places of interest in the area. On Sunday 29th August, we travelled to London and continued our tour.

The highlight of our visit was Windsor Castle. The castle was badly burnt, and this was the main reason that the public was allowed to visit the residences—Buckingham Palace and Windsor Castle—for a fee. This was the first time, in British history, that the public was allowed to visit the royal residence. Windsor Castle was like a little city unto itself. The castle is a very large and self-contained building complex. Within the enclosure are shops, stores, parks, theaters, a post office, schools, and amusement facilities.

On Monday, 30th August, we visited the city of Oxford. This was a most awesome and delightful experience. The main attraction in the city of Oxford is Oxford University. This is one of the oldest universities in the world. It was established in 1212. The architecture and beautiful artistic sculptures are impressive and breath taking. When university professors came to the university, students gathered around them to ask them questions and listen carefully to their speech and lectures. These professors are held in high regard by the entire community.

One of the greatest highlights of our visit to England occurred on Tuesday, 31st August. On this day we visited Buckingham Palace in London. Before entering the palace, everyone and everything were carefully scanned by an electronic scanner machine. The staircase that leads to Her Majesty's throne room has no visible means of support. It is constructed as if it were "flying."

I've never seen anything like that before or since that experience. The chandeliers were the largest and most exotic I have ever seen. The stair case to the throne room and the chandeliers were pure gold. Her Majesty's, the queen's, throne was pure gold, so was her royal scepter and sword that she uses in the function of her duties as the head of state. There were three different rooms—green, red and blue rooms—that were adjacent to the royal throne room. All the furniture, chandeliers, and crystals in the green room were green. This was also similar in the red room and in the blue room. Our visit to Buckingham Palace was very impressive, and will long be remembered.

Wednesday, September 1st, 1993, was the last day of our visit to England. We spent the day doing some last minute shopping in the city of High Wycombe. We purchased souvenirs for ourselves and family members and friends in the United States. The next day, Thursday, September 2nd, we made our way to Gatwick International Airport, and made the long trip back home to the United States. We had the unfortunate experience of discovering that most of the video pictures that we took with my VCR were scrambled and spoiled when we placed the VCR and everything else in our possession on a conveyer belt that were passed through a scanner at Buckingham Palace.

I returned to work at Rosewood Center after our vacation in the United Kingdom. On December 6th, 1993, I received some very distressing news. I was sent a letter from the Department of Human Resources, indicating that owing to budget reductions which have been imposed by the Department of Health and Mental Hygiene, the funding for the position I occupied would be discontinued effective March 18, 1994! "Through this letter you are hereby given a ninety (90) day notice that you will be laid off effective March 18, 1994." My family and I took this serious situation to the Lord in prayer. I started the process of seeking other employment. On January 3rd 1994, I received another letter that stated the following: "this is to inform you that your pending lay off scheduled for March 18, 1994 from the position of Licensed Practical Nurse II is being rescinded. Accordingly, you will continue your employment with Rosewood Center." Needless to say, my family and I were over-joyed in our thanks and gratitude to our Heavenly Father!

On June 10th, 1995, Cindy and I went on vacation for two (2) weeks. We visited the Caribbean and we sent Eliot and Sean to visit their grandparents in Berrien Springs, Michigan. We had a truly enjoyable time, sharing happy moments with relatives and friends. We visited some tourist sites, went to the beach, and took boat rides. We also attended church services on weekends. Inasmuch as we were visiting from the U.S., I was asked to preach the sermon on Saturday 17th and Sunday 18th, June 1995. This was a deep and moving spiritual experience for me. We had a safe and pleasant flight back to the United States, and on Monday 26th of June 1995, Cindy and I returned to work.

In November 1995 or January 1996 we received a promotional letter in the mail. The contents indicated that we, my wife and I, were being offered an all-expense-paid trip to the Bahamas. We had to pay our round trip airline ticket to Orlando, Florida. Our hotel accommodations and cruise to the Bahamas were all paid for by Carnival Cruise Lines. This was promoted by the time share incorporated. It took us a while to believe our good fortune, to be offered this opportunity. After praying about the matter, we decided to accept the offer. On Tuesday, June 11th 1996, Eliot and Sean flew to Berrien Springs, Michigan, to spend some time with their grandparents and other relatives (Cindy's folks) in Michigan. On Monday, June 24^{th,} we flew to Orlando, Florida. We had a good flight. We found our hotel, registered, and rested for the rest of the day. The next day we were picked up by limousine service and taken to the dock which was close to the Kennedy Space Center. We got on board the cruise ship and sailed to Freeport, Bahamas. On this trip we had lots of fun, food, and excitement.

We boarded the cruise ship, the Dolphin, on June 25th, and started sailing for the Bahamas at about 4:00 p.m. At about 6:00 p.m. there was a security drill. All passengers were lined up on deck in two rows. A member of the staff demonstrated security measures that must be taken in the event of a fire, or any other emergency situation, that may occur on the ship during the trip. We were also given tickets and directions to the many eating places on the ship. Cindy and I went to a small dining area and ordered our dinner for the evening. Our surrounding was beautifully decorated with soft music in the background. We then toured the upper deck of the ship. There was so much to see that we did not complete the entire tour that day. We ended our visit at the large pool on the main deck. The music was provided by steel drums, calypso and Latin music, singing and dancing. A memorable experience transpired! A woman dancer on stage asked different people to join her on stage to dance with her. She pointed to me and asked me to join her on stage. I told her I do not dance. She continued to insist that I join her and started to make her way in my direction. I started to walk away. She followed after me. As she got closer I started to run, and she started running after me. Cindy thought the situation was funny and started to laugh. After a little while, the woman stopped chasing me and returned on stage. We had a long and tiring day and retired for the night about 11:00 p.m. Even though we were tired, sleep did not come easily owing to the full and exciting day that transpired.

The next day, Wednesday, June 26, when we woke up that morning, we were in Freeport, Bahamas. We were given three different options of places to visit that day. My wife Cindy chose to go shopping in Freeport, and we visited the botanical gardens and other places of interest. We took many pictures of people and places we visited, and purchased several souvenirs. We returned to the ship about 3:00 or 4:00 p.m. that day, in order to prepare for the Captain's Ball. The Captain's Ball was truly a special and memorable event. The ball started at 7:00 p.m. Passengers were assigned to tables by a prescribed system. At our table were a young couple form Ney York and a middle aged couple from California. Entertainment for the evening was provided by various singing groups and performers. We were served a four-course dinner—an appetizer, soup or salad, the main course and dessert. Everyone were elegantly dressed for the occasion. The entertainment and dancing continued hours after the dinner was over. Cindy and I had a splendid and delightful evening. We retired for the night, and the next day, Thursday June 27, we arrived at Port Canaveral in Orlando, Florida, U.S.A. At 9:00 a.m., we were picked up by Able Transportation Service and taken to our hotel. On Friday June 28, we visited Walt Disney World. This was a very enjoyable experience. We attended aquatic performances by humans and dolphins and other sea creatures. We saw performances by groups from around the world.

On Sunday, June 20, we took a chartered bus to Daytona Beach. The Holiday Inn, in which we stayed, was directly on the beach. From our hotel balcony we saw people swimming in the Atlantic Ocean during the day and night. We spent that Sunday touring the board-walk and the many shops, café and other places of interest along the board-walk. The temperature was 105 degrees and very humid. Many young girls and guys visited shops and cafes almost naked, because of the heat and humidity. Sunday afternoon we attended an obligatory meeting for a time share. We also attended a similar meeting for time share in Orlando. Sunday night we took the chartered bus back to Orlando. The next stop on our itinerary was New Orleans, Louisiana. Cindy decided that she wanted to return home to Maryland because she was becoming very tired, probably owing to lack of sleep. On Tuesday July 2nd, we took a 7:00 p.m. flight back to Baltimore, Maryland. On Tuesday August 6th, Eliot and Sean returned home from their vacation in Berrien Springs, Michigan.

My sister Merle continued to keep me informed concerning our dad's health and well-being. He was now 84 years old, and had been experiencing many ailments and bodily dysfunctions. He had an extended history of arthritic problems and difficulties with ambulation as a result. He also had difficulties with his eyesight. He had high blood pressure for an extended period of time. In July 1997, he was admitted into the hospital for blood test, due to high blood pressure and also for difficulty with ambulation and balance. On October 29th, dad went home to meet the Lord. My sister, Merle, informed me of his passing, and I immediately made preparations to attend the funeral. Cindy was unable to get the time off from her job and was unable to accompany me to the funeral. This was considered a special situation, and I was given ten (10) days off from my job to attend my dad's funeral. On Friday October 31st, 1997, I boarded an American Airline Flight that took me to my destination in the Caribbean. Dad's funeral was conducted in the Ashton Seventh-day Adventist church on Sunday, November 2nd 1997. The family requested that I deliver the eulogy, and I did. Many family members and friends were in attendance at the church and at the cemetery for his burial. After spending special time with relatives and close friends, I caught a flight on November 6th, and returned to the United States.

    Owing to the demands of my job at Rosewood Center and my inability to get release time (time off work) to continue the nursing program, I had to make a decision. I worked in Maryland state government for seven (7) years and had achieved tenured (permanent) status. On February 20th, 1998, I resigned my nursing position at Rosewood to pursue the nursing (RN) program at Catonsville Community College, on a full-time basis. I was working with a private nursing agency before I resigned my position with the state of Maryland, and I continued working with this agency while I attended nursing school.

    After a successful interview process, I got another job with the state of Maryland. I worked as an addiction counselor in the Howard County health department. I started my new job on Wednesday 23rd, September, 1998. This was a very challenging and rewarding job experience. My duties involved conducting counseling and intake sessions with individuals and groups. There were staff meetings at least once each week. At these meetings, the six members of my counseling team met and talked about particular clients that were assigned. One of the reasons that this was done was so that the team members would be informed and knowledgeable, in the event that a given client or clients were reassigned to a different counselor. I conducted four (4) different groups: (1) Individual counseling, (2) Group counseling, (3) Family counseling, and (4) Parent group counseling. My group sessions were comprised of students who were drug repeat offenders, for the most part. They were sent to Howard County Health Department, addiction program by different high schools in Howard County. They were sent there for treatment and education instead of being introduced to the correctional and legal system. This was a 28-day, mandatory program. A urine test for the presence of drugs could be requested by the counselors at any time. If the client refused to submit to the test, it was considered to be an automatic positive result. The counselor had to then notify the client's (student) probation officer of the situation. The group sessions also involved oral and written assignments. Clients were expected to pay for a certain part of their treatment (a sliding scale system). If one of my clients had a court appointment, I was sometimes required to accompany that client to the court appointment. I was assigned three (3) high schools: Glenelg, Wilde Lake, and Long Reach, in Howard County. My duties and task were to meet with the student support team in each school and be part of the therapeutic process. Appropriate students who needed help, were assigned to the Howard County treatment program.

  Working as a counselor in the addiction treatment program was one of the most rewarding events of my work experiences. The process of recovery, healing, and restoration to wholeness, has truly been a transformational event to observe and witness. Owing to a poor home environment or some unfortunate occurrence at school, an adolescent could find himself or herself practicing a given behavior that becomes an addiction. This situation could bring about feelings of guilt, shame, and loss of self-worth. This state of affairs often leads to self-defeating attitudes and negative behavior patterns. When a student entered the program there would often be a lack of hope, trust, and a negative disposition. The group process is a wonderful therapeutic tool for achieving a satisfactory result. As a client listened, observed, and eventually participated in group discussions and other events, the individual came to understand that he or she was not unique or alone regarding the problem that he or she was experiencing. As a result, hope, heling and recovery began to occur. As the client continued in the program, greater confidence was developed. Eventually, attitude and behavior changes for the better were achieved. Many students were restored to good and regular academic and social citizenship in their homes and schools. The twelve-step program, as employed by Alcoholics Anonymous, formed an integral component of the counseling process. Behavior modification techniques were also utilized as an educational and therapeutic tool. The following cases were two of my clients that participated in the treatment program at the Howard County health department. These cases were a typical representation of the clients who were sent to the treatment program for help with addictions and other dysfunctions.

Andrew M. Roberts (pseudonym) was a 17-year old, single male who was referred for substance abuse counseling by the Department of Juvenile Justice. He was arrested in 1996 for drug paraphernalia and was expelled from school in 1997 for smoking and abusing marijuana. On July 25th, 1998, he was arrested for possession of a dangerous substance (marijuana). He was scheduled to appear in court on November 19, 1998. Andrew was a student at Howard High school. He was in the 12th grade at the time of this report. His academic work was average in performance. He indicated that school provided him an opportunity to learn and eventually to go to college and he wanted to pursue a degree in communications in order to qualify for a job with a radio station. Andrew lived with both of his parents, his sister, who was 20 years old, and a younger brother. He was born in Howard County. He smoked one pack of cigarettes and cannabis (marijuana) a day. He denied that he was a habitual user of alcohol. This client reported that he suffered from allergies, asthma and was referred by his physician for depression, sometime in the past. He indicated that none of his presenting conditions needed to be treated at the present time. Andrew stated that he did not have any sexual interest at the time of this report, but he had been sexually active and did utilize a condom as a protective device.

A treatment plan was devised for Andrew that committed him to successfully completing a minimum of a 26-week education and treatment program. He was also required to submit to at least twelve separate urine specimens for urinalysis. Also, in order to remedy family relationship problems, the family was encouraged to attend a minimum of four (4) family counseling sessions.

Assessment and prognosis of the counseling process

It was recommended that Andrew should complete a minimum of 26 weeks of counseling. He received an educational based treatment regimen with random urine screens. It was explained to Andrew and his mother that any positive urine screens would add more time to treatment. The SASSI was used as a diagnostic tool and the POSIT was used as a screening device during the intake process. The diagnostic impression was alcohol and marijuana abuse. The consequence for continued drug use and abuse would be referred back to the Department of Juvenile Justice, and placement in an appropriate program. Andrew did not report any problems that existed with his parents or his brother and sister. There were indications of previous cannabis and alcohol abuse. He was expelled from school and was arrested for the possession and use of illicit drugs. Andrew indicated that he wanted to give consent to no one regarding the issue of identifying information about him as a client in the counseling program.

The following case history concerned another client whom I also counseled individually in a group setting. Melissa Robinson (a pseudonym) was a 17-year-old, single female who was referred to the drug treatment center for substance abuse counseling by her high school counselor, for marijuana and alcohol abuse. Melissa attended Howard High School, and graduated in 1999. She stated that her grades were good and she received honors in English and Social Studies. She was the first born of her three siblings. Her parents were divorced on June 28, 1997. Melissa and her mother had a very stormy relationship, and she moved out of her mother's house soon after she graduated from high school. Melissa indicated that what she most liked about school was "to see my friends, my guidance counselor and math." She stated that she wanted to get a steady job after she graduated from high school. She said that her father, grandfather and several other family members were alcoholics. She also said that as a child, the fighting between her parents made her feel distraught and discouraged. She did not feel neglected as an adolescent. When she was seven (7) years old, Melissa jumped off a balcony and injured her left leg. She was taken to the hospital, where an x-ray and a blood test were done. She later had a complete physical examination. Melissa indicated that she learned about sexual matters from television, her parents, and school. She did have a boyfriend and had been sexually active with him. She used prophylactic devices and was aware of how AIDS and HIV are transmitted.

Assessment and Prognosis of the Counseling Process

The counseling team recommended that Melissa complete a minimum of 26 weeks of counseling. This included the completion of an educational series and random urine tests to ascertain a drug free status and attendance at a 12-step Narcotics Anonymous program. The SASSI was used as a diagnosis tool, and the POSIT was utilized as a screening device during the intake process. The diagnostic impression was marijuana and alcohol abuse.

Working as a counselor in the addiction treatment program was rewarding, but there were also obstacles and challenges relating to the issue of training and commitment to the program.

Chapter 6

Travel and Challenges

"I will teach you the way that you should go; I will keep my eye on you and guide you along safe paths." —Psalm 32:8 (The Clear Word)

In July, 2000 there was an important convention that was held in Toronto, Canada. We decided to attend as a family. On July 5th, 2000, we boarded a U.S. Airways aircraft and traveled to Toronto, Canada. After picking up our Enterprise Rent-a-Car, which was close to Toronto International Airport, we traveled to my (Zeph's) uncle's home in Toronto, where we stayed for the duration of the visit to the religious convention. We had a wonderful time visiting relatives, friends, places, and we made some new acquaintances of people from different parts of the world.

On July 6th, 2000, at 5:00 p.m., my wife Cindy and I attended my University alumni reception at the Horizon Room in the CN Tower, the tallest building in Canada at that time. The dinner and the fellowship were memorable events. Our journey back to the U.S. involved an extraordinary experience. As we embarked on our flight from Toronto, Canada, to Maryland, USA, I placed one of our carry-on bags in the over-head compartment. We had a beautiful flight. As we disembarked, I took my carry-on luggage in the over-head compartment, not observing that there was another piece of luggage that was almost identical to mine. When I got home and opened the bag, I discovered that it belonged to the female flight attendant who was on the same flight from Toronto. This was a big mistake! But this was a worse disaster for the flight attendant! This piece of luggage contained her credit cards, her passport, hundreds of dollars, and the keys to her car, that was parked at the airport in Toronto. I immediately contacted the airport in Baltimore, Maryland. They contacted the airport personnel in Toronto. I called and spoke to the flight attendant's mother in Canada. She told me that her daughter's boyfriend will pick her up from the airport in Canada. She said that her daughter wanted me to mail her luggage directly to their home address in Canada, and she would mail my luggage to my address in the U.S. The flight attendant called and let me know that she was overjoyed to have received all the contents that were in her luggage. I told her that I was also pleased to receive my luggage. I'm convinced that the Lord providentially intervened in this experience.

In July 2001, my family—Cindy, Eliot and Sean—and I traveled to Trinidad to pay a visit to my family and friends. We were picked up at Piarco International Airport by Mr. John Thompson, the husband of my cousin Mona Thompson. They are both teachers by profession. We drove from the airport to their home in the town of Tarcariqua, and was welcomed by other members of the Thompson family. They have two sons and a daughter. For quite a few days we did shopping and visited some relatives and friends living in different towns and cities in Trinidad. The local church officials learned that I was visiting from the U.S., and asked if I would be willing to preach the sermon for the church service. I gladly accepted the privilege and honor to serve in this way. This event was truly an exciting and satisfying experience. Sunday afternoon we went to the beach for the entire day. This was delightful indeed.

A very interesting incident occurred, as Cindy and I were shopping in Port-of-Spain, the capital of Trinidad. We were shopping in a store that sold various articles of clothing and accessories. As we were shopping, a man ran into the store from off the street, snatched merchandise and ran out of the store and up the street! He came close to Cindy, where she was shopping! She became alarmed and petrified! I tried my best to console and comfort her, as she was upset by this experience. The store manager called the police and reported the incident, but we don't know if the thief was apprehended! We immediately left the store and carried on with the rest of our itinerary. We thanked the Lord for his protection and watch care! Other than this unfortunate event, we had a wonderful visit. At the end of our stay, we boarded an American Airlines flight and returned to our home in Maryland, USA.

We returned from our Caribbean trip and also returned to our jobs. At this time I was working at Sheppard Pratt Hospital in Towson, MD, as a psychiatric nurse. The work was challenging and rewarding. One of the most powerful and life changing events in American history occurred while I was working at Sheppard Pratt Hospital. An employee who was working on the dual diagnosis unit shouted, "A plane just flew into one of the Trade Center towers in New York City." A crowd quickly gathered around the television set in the lounge area on the fifth floor. As everyone watched in amazement the scene became more fearful as we saw a second plane fly into the second Trade Center building. By this time everyone knew that the United States was under a terrorist attack. Many people were terrified and petrified. The other nurse with whom I was working became so anxious and stressed that she wanted to go home. She said "I really would like to go home."

I responded "we are the only two nurses that are working on this unit (dual diagnosis) at this time and we cannot leave these patients." As she continued to look at the events that were transpiring on the TV she became more afraid and apprehensive. As a result of the 911 terrorist attack, we admitted several patients to the hospital who were suffering from mental and emotional difficulties because of this event.

At the end of Fall in 2001, I received a letter in the mail concerning a promotional offer. It concerned a trip for two people (my wife and I) to travel free to one of three destinations: Hawaii, Cancun, Mexico, or the Bahamas. The hotel room had to be paid for by the participants. My wife and I decided to accept the offer to go to Hawaii. We made preparation and booked our passage on

Delta Airlines for Hawaii. On September 2nd, 2002, my wife Cindy and I departed Baltimore Washington International Airport for Honolulu, Hawaii. Our journey started at 8:45 am. We made stops in Atlanta, Georgia, and Los Angeles, California. We arrived in Honolulu, Hawaii at 5:12 p.m. On our way to the hotel in Waikiki, our rented car broke down. We tried to make contact with AUU, the car rental company, but were unsuccessful. The owner of a gun shop business, in front of whose establishment the rented car broke down, saw our plight and came to our rescue. He called the car rental company on his cell phone, and they brought us another vehicle that was much better. We thanked the gentleman, Mr. Park, profusely for his kind assistance. We also thanked our almighty Father, for His loving kindness and His tender mercies. We were very glad to get to our hotel, The Waikiki Beachcomber, after a long day of travel.

On Tuesday, September 3, 2002, we left our hotel room at 10:00 a.m. We made the reservation for a bus tour of the island of Oahu, for the next day, Wednesday. We then visited a shopping plaza and purchased some Hawaiian tee shirts, post cards, key chains, and other souvenirs. We had lunch at the plaza, did some more shopping, and then returned to the hotel and rested. At about 7 p.m., we went out and got something to eat. After walking around the plaza and visiting the sites we returned to our hotel, watched television for a while and retired for the night.

On Wednesday, September 4, we woke up at about 6:00 a.m., had breakfast, and caught a bus at 7:30 a.m. in our hotel lobby. This bus took us to the tour bus. We experienced amazing sights of mountains, valleys, and sea coast. The bus stopped at a restaurant and everyone was able to buy dinner. Everyone ate, returned to the bus, and the tour continued. We stopped at breathtaking look-out sights of canyons, valleys, and mountains. The tour afforded us the opportunity to take many beautiful and memorable pictures. Along the way we stopped at the Dole Pineapple Plantation. There we had pineapple ice cream and purchased souvenirs.

Our tour guide and bus driver's name was Leroy. He had an amazing and incredible story. He was from Wisconsin. He told the passengers on the tour bus his story: "I was visiting Hawaii, with my wife about 5 years ago. While on vacation we fell in love with Hawaii. We decided to get jobs and live here! My wife and I decided that she should return to Wisconsin and sell our house and all our belongings and then return to Hawaii. Her parents dissuaded her from carrying out this plan and she stayed in Wisconsin, and never came back to Hawaii." Leroy also told us of some favorite Hawaiian cuisine. He said "two of our favorite dishes are called pee pee, and poo-poo [pupu]." Everyone on the tour bus broke out in uncontrollable laughter!

The bus tour was truly a memorable event. On Thursday, September 5, 2002, our plan was to visit the famous Polynesian Cultural Center in Honolulu. We took the tour bus, The Superstar, and made our first stop at the Mormon temple visitors center. We got off the bus and visited certain parts of the temple. An interesting incident transpired during our visit. A young Mormon woman who was our tour guide wanted us to go into the inner part of the temple, my wife Cindy and I told her that we were not comfortable doing that, owing to our Christian beliefs. We were surprised when she became upset and disappointed, because of our unwillingness to go along with the visitation program. After leaving this event, the tour bus took us to the Polynesian Cultural Center. This was truly an extraordinary experience. There were boat rides on small lakes, shows about cultural dances by dancers from Fiji, Tonga, The Solomon Islands, and other dancers from native islands in the South Pacific. We had the opportunity to have our pictures taken with several of the performers at the cultural center.

Friday, September 6, we spent in a leisurely way, and did some shopping and sight-seeing at a local mall called the Alamoana. After having a nice lunch at the mall, Cindy and I returned to our hotel to rest and to prepare for a dinner to which we were invited. We had a very interesting and delightful visit. On Saturday, September 7, we attended a small Seventh-day Adventist church on the outskirts of the city on Honolulu. While Cindy and I sat in the congregation, a gentleman tapped me on my shoulder and asked me if I would be willing to preach the sermon that day. After some thought I decided to accept the honor and the challenge. After the service, there was a beautiful potluck dinner and Christian fellowship. Most of the Hawaiian people are very gracious, affable, and hospitable. We returned to our hotel and spent the rest of the day relaxing, in preparation for a long trip back home the next day. After travelling for about thirteen hours, we finally arrived in Baltimore at 3:53 p.m., on Tuesday, 10th September, 2002.

It was a bright and sunny Wednesday afternoon on April 19^{th,} 2006. I was travelling north on Route 27 in Westminster, the town in which I resided. The cars that were in front of me slowed down. In my rear view mirror I saw a green Jeep Cherokee, 2000. The driver was travelling fast. I thought for sure that when the driver observed that the traffic was slowing down, he will do the same. He did not slow down because he was talking to the other two passengers who were travelling with him, instead of paying attention to the traffic in front of him. He ran his vehicle into the back of my car. I experienced a terrible jolt, a terrific headache, and dizziness. I slumped over the steering wheel. The young man jumped out of his jeep! "Are you all right, would you like me to call an ambulance?" About 15 or 20 minutes went by.

After I slowly regained my composure, I responded, "I first want to try to contact my wife, so she can take me to the hospital." I was also able to obtain pertinent information from Mr. Justin A. Oliver, the driver of the 2000 Jeep Cherokee. A little later, family members of the driver and two police officers (a man and a woman) arrived on the scene of the accident. An accident report was eventually prepared by officer Debbie Zittel. She did not want to prepare a formal report nor issue a traffic citation to Mr. Justin

Oliver. At my request, the police officer finally prepared an accident report. She asked me if I wanted to go to the hospital by ambulance. I told her that my wife would take me to the hospital. My wife arrived at the scene of the accident and then drove me to Carroll Hospital Center. We were taken to the Triage unit for immediate attention. A medical history, physical exam, and an x-ray were done. The results were satisfactory. Thank the Lord for His loving kindness and His tender mercies! Later that day I was discharged from the hospital and my wife took me home. While I was in the hospital, I was given two Advils for neck and back pain. I was also given a prescription for medication: Flexeril 10mg, to relax my muscles, Percocet 5/305, for pain and an orthopedic referral.

    In June, my mom, Mavis Ambrose, was visiting her children in the USA and Canada. The few days that mom spent with us in our home were very special indeed. After spending many years apart studying and trying to make my mark in the world, I finally got the deep satisfaction and delight of spending some alone time with mom in our home with my family. Cindy and I made meals for her and took her out to visit different sights and places. I was able to have conversations with her about questions I had always wanted to ask her about my childhood, my dad, and other family concerns, but never had the opportunity. This was truly quality time that was well spent. After mom left our house, she went to Canada to visit with my other brothers and sisters and other family members who lived in Canada. It was as if she knew that her final days on this earth were coming to an end, and she was saying her final goodbye.

    While mom was visiting with my brother Ishmael at his residence in Canada, she reportedly had a stroke, fell, and struck her head. She was taken to the hospital, bud did not recover. She subsequently died as a result of that accident. My family and I travelled to Canada and attended the funeral. I was asked by the family to deliver the eulogy. The following remarks are a summary of the eulogy I delivered:

"Today I will see my mom in this present world for the last time. I plan to see her when I get to heaven! My mom has had a profound effect on my life. She taught me and my brothers and sisters to be good and compassionate people. As children, mom taught us God's word and how to honor and love Him. To this day my favorite breakfast is hot cereal. She made hot cereal from scratch every other day. This was also one of her favorite breakfast items. Mom taught her children many Christian songs. Mom had a beautiful singing voice and she sang constantly. I fell in love with music because of her. I remembered her telling us 'When you sing, your work becomes easier and lighter, so sing while you work, angry or playing.' Mom was a very kind and caring person. She was a good cook. I learned to cook from her and my dad. She also had a phenomenal memory! A few weeks before she died, she sang several songs and recited many portions of the Bible verbatim from memory. I inherited her good memory and this ability was very helpful in my studies.

"Mom passed on to her children those qualities—roots and wings—that made it possible for us to live with meaning and purpose. Roots and wings are two of the most valuable gifts that parents can give to their children. Roots has to do with values. Transcendent spiritual values that are based on divine principles, that are found in God's word, the Bible. Examples are The Ten Commandments and The Beatitudes. Living by these principles will help us to be a success in this world and the next. The gift of wings has to do with goals, aspirations and an attitude of achievement. Mom always encouraged us to aim high and do our best. Two months before she travelled to Canada, mom spent some beautiful and valuable times with my family and me at our home in Maryland. My wife, Cindy, took a week's vacation from her job to spend with mom. Cindy loved mom, and mom loved Cindy and our two sons. Mom liked to play with Cindy's hair.

"Goodbye my dearest mother! May the Lord bless you and keep you! May He cause his face to shine upon you. May He lift up his countenance upon you and be gracious unto you, until we meet on the other side of eternity."

Attending a funeral forces a person to have deep reflections concerning important and critical issues about the meaning and purpose of life. When a funeral is the death of a close loved one such as a mother or father, the reflections and thought processes becomes deeper and wider in scope. This situation brings one face to face with one's own mortality. Death is seen as a real part of the life process! I experienced this situation at my mother's funeral.

In 2007 my wife and I found ourselves in a serious and dire predicament. We owed $53,000 in credit cards and other debts. We took this situation to the Lord in serious prayer and supplication. We were able to get into a consumer counseling program that helped to consolidate our debts. We tried to refinance our house, but were unsuccessful. During this time, I started working with World Financial Group, a life and health insurance and mortgage company. This work opportunity was truly a providence from the Lord. Although I was a new employee with this company and I was deficient in some financial requirements, I felt impressed to apply for a loan to refinance our home. We offered fervent prayers to the Lord and he answered our prayers in the affirmative. Our house was refinanced and the equity was used to liquidate the entire debt of $53,000! Praise the Lord for His loving kindness!

I worked with World Financial Group for about two years. I travelled to the company's headquarters in San Jose, California, for meetings and a big convention. This was an exciting and eye-opening experience. For the first time in my life I rubbed shoulders and associated with millionaires. The company was owned by a gentleman of Asian background, Xvan, and most of the employees were Asians. Their aspirations and achievements truly embodied the immigrant spirit. Education and hard work were highly prized. As a Christian I was amazed at the total immersion of everyone in this materialistic enterprise. It seemed as if everyone lived for the almighty dollar! There were no apparent over-riding concerns about spiritual matters. Greed and selfish desires were evident, working in this environment, a person can, if not careful, lose sight of moral principles and values in the pursuit of riches and wealth.

In July 2007, Cindy and I visited California for nine (9) days. We spent a few days with our son Sean in northern California and then attended a business convention, conducted by World Financial Group, in southern California (Anaheim). We also visited a relative, Loma Linda University, and the city of Riverside where our hotel was located.

On Sunday February 3rd 2008, Cindy and I travelled to Orlando, Florida for a health conference, sponsored by the North and Inter-American Divisions of the Seventh-day Adventist Church. I attended this seminar in the capacity of director of the health ministry in my local church. The summit conference was conducted in the Sheraton Hotel in Orlando, Florida. There were many people from throughout north America, the Caribbean, and Latin America. The sessions were very informative and intense. Leaders from the health departments of both divisions were the presenters. The fundamental thesis and philosophy of the conference was that health was part of the same continuum as the gospel of salvation. The information that was shared, emphasized that the human body, mind, and spirit is a unitary whole. When one part is affected, the whole body will be impacted as well. When the spiritual part of man is whole, this benefits the entire human organism. When the spiritual emphasis is omitted, the mental and physical aspects are incomplete and are likely to suffer dysfunction. Factual information and research findings were offered to support this position. There is a wonderful sympathy that exist between the spiritual, mental and physical aspects of the human personality. The holy scriptures states that we humans are "fearfully and wonderfully made" in the image of the Almighty Creator.

In her book, *Man of Destiny*, p. 671, Ellen G. White made the following observation: "It is by the Holy Spirit that the heart is made pure. Through the Spirit, the believer becomes a part-taker of the divine nature. Christ has given His spirit as a divine power to overcome all hereditary and cultivated tendency to evil, and to impress His own character upon His church." The mental health literature suggests that a person's beliefs and attitudes are founded in four (4) human activities: (1) Thinking, (2) Feeling, (3) Behaving, and (4) Interacting. Firmly anchored attitudes are resistant to change. In this theory of cognitive dissonance, Feastinger suggests that if an individual engages in behavior that is inconsistent with his beliefs, he will be sufficiently motivated to resolve the conflict by changing his beliefs to coincide with his behavior. Biases and prejudices are caused by lack of tolerance for individual differences. Many people feel uncomfortable or threatened by people who have different views, skin color, dress codes, or patterns of social interactions. Some fears are caused by lack of exposure, rigidity of thinking, fear of the unknown, avoidance of risks, and other self-defeating behaviors that contribute to an individual's intolerance. To change a belief system that one has operated with for many years, requires learning new information, working hard at acquiring new behaviors and establishing new ways of thinking. Biases are not changed simply because one believes one should be different, Biases are changed by diligent effort and self-examination. The first step is to acknowledge our biases and then admit that they have an impact on our behavior and our interaction with other people. Albert Ellis proposed that changing one's beliefs and attitudes will result in a change of behavior. According to rational-emotive theory, it is the way one thinks about experiences that governs behavior, rather than the other way around. An eclectic perspective sees the process as circular in nature, each part influencing the other. Another useful perspective is family systems theory. This approach integrates the biological, psychological, social and environmental aspects of development. A family system paradigm recognizes that an individual's behavior is the product of many varied forces and contexts. A client's immediate family is usually the most important of these contexts. Family mental health counselors and therapists focus on family interactions as the primary source of meaning and influence, and therefore a source of power to produce and sustain positive change.

Jesus promised that the Holy Spirit would do a special work of guiding God's people in all truth (John 14:20; 16:12-15). Although human counselors cannot literally penetrate the mind of their clients, they can profoundly influence their thinking. But the Holy Spirit is able to enter our innermost being. And if we consent to the operation of His grace, He will transform our thoughts and enable us to guide our clients therapeutically. As the Christian mental health counselor or psychologist continues to submit himself to Christ, the heart becomes united with His heart the will is merged in His will, the mind becomes one with His mind and the thoughts are brought into captivity to Him. In this way the Holy Spirit illumines the Christian counselor with wisdom and understanding, as he guides his clients towards healing and wholeness.

Research has shown that people who attend religious services more than once a week, live on average, seven years longer than those who do not. A 1998 study by Duke University Medical Center doctors, Harold Koeing and David Larson, found that those people who attended church weekly were not as likely to be hospitalized, and when they were, they did not spend as much time in the hospital as those who went to church less frequently. Some of these findings that were demonstrated during the seminar, can be attributed to the fact that church goers were less likely to smoke, drink or engage in risky sexual behavior, and they usually had a network of social support. In 1995, a Dartmouth University Medical School study, found that patients who were comforted by their faith had three times the chance of being alive six months after open-heart surgery than patients who found no comfort in religion.

In 1999, a Duke University study of nearly 4,000 older adults found that attendance at a house of worship is related to lower rates of depression and anxiety. Dr. Matthews, an internist that practiced in Washington D.C., observed that his patients wanted more from him than a physical diagnosis. His grandfather was a missionary and he himself was a person of faith. When taking the medical histories of his patients, he will often ask them about their religious faith and belief, which greatly determined his treatment approach.

One of Dr. Matthews' patients, a biotech consultant who was chronically ill with an autoimmune condition, said, "It's as if he has a deeper range of support." At 47-years-old, this patient had surgery to replace an aortic valve, had Crohn's Disease identified in his intestinal tract, and lived with arthritis in his joints. Living with degenerative, life-threating illness had not been easy. He said that he had managed to get along the past six years by becoming more spiritual. Dr. Matthews occasionally wrote scripture references for this patient on a prescription pad and referred him to spiritual resources. In her book, *Health and Happiness* (page 175), E. G. White made the following statement: "The power of the will is not valued as it should be. Let the will be kept awake and rightly directed, and it will impart energy to the whole being, and will be a wonderful aid in the maintenance of health. It is a power also in dealing with disease. Exercised in the right direction, it will control the imagination and be a potent means of resisting and overcoming disease of both mind and body. By the exercise of the willpower in placing themselves in a right relation to life, patients can do much to co-operate with the physician's efforts for their recovery. There are thousands who can recover health if they will. The Lord does not want them to be sick. He desires them to be well and happy, and they should make up their minds to be well. Often, invalids can resist disease, simply by refusing to yield to ailments and settle down in a state of inactivity. Rising above their aches and pains, let them engage in useful employment and the free use of air and sunlight, many an emaciated invalid might recover health and strength." For the duration of the conference Cindy and I stayed with Uncle John and Aunt Pat at their home in the town of Apopka, a suburb of the city of Orlando, Florida. Even though the seminar took up most of the week, we were able to spend some delightful and quality time with family members. This conference was a very satisfying and blessed experience.

In October 2008, Cindy and I travelled to Berrien Springs, Michigan, in order to attend April Nelson's (Cindy's niece) wedding. It was truly delightful to visit with many family members again. This was a special event for me, personally. I held April in my arms when she was a baby! Therefore, to witness this very important step in her life's journey was a momentous and delightful event indeed. Her future husband's name was Jordon Miller. They had a beautiful garden wedding. The groom's family were pleasant and delightful to get acquainted with and to know.

In the year 2009 I faced a difficult challenge. I had to make an important decision concerning a benign cyst that was growing on the left side of my nose. After consulting with my wife and physician, and the completion of pre-operative procedures, a date for the surgery was scheduled for August 7th, 2009, at 1:00 p.m. Only local anesthesia was necessary, and the entire procedure went well. Thank the Lord for His goodness and grace!

Chapter 7
Reflections

The preceding experiences of my journey compel me to pause and reflect on the grace and goodness of the Lord. In the twenty-third (23rd) psalm, the psalmist David identifies with the Good Shepherd. King David wrote this poem when he was an old man. As a shepherd boy, he spent a great deal of the time with his sheep. David knew his sheep and his sheep knew him. As he looked over his life, as an old man, he observed that the Lord took care of him, in a similar way that he took care of his sheep, when he was a young many. He was like a sheep and the Lord was his shepherd.

The following story was told of the Shepherd's Psalm. There was an oratory contest about the 23rd Psalm. The last two finalist in the contest were a professional actor and an elderly gentleman. After the professional actor finished reciting the Shepherd Psalm, he was given a standing ovation for several minutes by the audience. The elderly gentlemen followed, and took his place on the stage. When he was finished reciting the psalm, there were no applause and no standing ovation! There was only silence throughout the auditorium! There were no dry eyes in the audience! Many asked what made the difference in the audience's response. The actor returned to the stage. He said, "It is obvious by your standing ovation that you were pleased by my knowledge and rendition of the Shepherd's Psalm. However, while I know the Psalm very well, this elderly gentleman knows the Shepherd himself, personally. This accounted for the difference in your response."

The gift of God's love is the foundation and source of His grace and our identity. The scriptures talk about the mystery of the

Trinity, the mystery of the incarnation, the mystery of immortality and the mystery of divine grace! The virtue and quality of divine grace, unlike love, justice, or mercy, is a unilateral transaction—it flows in only one direction, from God to human beings. The scriptures states that while we were yet sinners, Christ died for us. His sacrifice is based on His love and our need, not on our goodness or our righteousness. In the familiar story recorded in John 4:4-26, the apostle John states, "Jesus had to go through Samaria." This even was probably foreordained before the foundation of the world. This story is one of the most powerful illustrations of divine grace that is found in the holy scriptures. The Samaritan woman had come to the well to draw water, and her curiosity was increased when Jesus told her that He had water that was much better than the water from Jacob's well. The record stated that the Samaritan woman came to draw water about the sixth hour of the day. This was the middle of the day, when the sun was very hot. The normal times that woman came to the well to draw water were during the morning and evening hours, when the sun was just rising or just setting. However, this woman came at midday because she wanted to avoid coming in contact with anyone else in her community. She was a woman of disreputable character and social standing in her community. Jesus asked this Samaritan woman for a drink of water. A respectable Jewish Rabbi may perchance converse briefly with a Jewish woman, but absolutely not with a Samaritan woman of such ill repute. By conversing with this woman, Jesus revealed the nature of divine grace. He came to seek and to save and empower lost people. God's grace is more than justice and more than mercy. He avails to us the full measure of His riches in glory. Jesus' request for a drink of water was very startling and surprising to this woman. Jesus went further and deeper, and offered her living water that will quench her thirst forever. This experience was almost too much for the woman to comprehend and assimilate. She queried, "Sir, you have nothing to draw with and the well is deep, where can you get this living water?" The woman observed that Jesus had no bucket, no rope, or any kind of equipment with which to get water from a deep well, yet because of the certainty, confidence and conviction with which He spoke, she believed the words of Jesus.

In verse 13 of John chapter 4, Jesus went still deeper in helping her to understand the meaning of this living water that He was offering to her. Jesus continued, "everyone who drinks this water in Jacob's well, will be thirsty again, but whoever drinks the water that I give him or her will never thirst. Indeed, the water I give him or her will become a spring of water welling up to eternal life." The woman said to Jesus, "Sir give me this water so that I won't get thirsty and have to keep coming here to draw water."

Jesus told her, "go call your husband and come back." Before this woman or any other sinner can receive the living water of God, the Holy Spirit, the scriptures said that we must confess our sins, and He is faithful and just to forgive us our sins and cleanse us from all unrighteousness.

The woman confessed, "I have no husband."

Jesus said to her, as he revealed to her the secrets of her heart and life. "You are right when you say you have no husband. The fact is you have had five husbands, and the man you now have is not your husband. What you have just said is quite true!" The Holy Spirit revealed to this woman, that this man, this Jewish rabbi called Jesus Christ, was no ordinary man.

"Sir," the woman said, "I can see that you are a prophet." At this point we see that the woman (Satan through the woman) tried to change the focus and spiritual nature of the subject matter. This woman was about to receive the Holy Spirit, and her commission as a Christian missionary. She said "Our fathers worship on this mountain, but you Jews claim that the place where we must worship is in Jerusalem."

At this point, Jesus introduced a new dimension in Christian theological thinking. Jesus declared, "believe me, woman, a time is coming when you will worship the Father neither on this mountain nor in Jerusalem. You Samaritans worship what you do not know; we worship what we do know, for salvation is from the Jews. Yet a time is coming and has now come, when the true worshiper will worship the Father in spirit and truth." Here we see perhaps for the first time in Jesus' ministry, the introduction of the doctrine of divine grace as a state of mind and heart, in which the Holy Spirit dwells, as opposed to a physical place like Jerusalem or any other place of worship on earth. Jesus continues by saying that God desires, and is pleased to be worshiped by those who are committed and sincere in heart, mind and spirit. God is spirit and His worshipers must worship in spirit, and in truth. The woman said, "I know that Messiah (the Christ) is coming, when he comes, he will explain everything to us."

There are many people who are not aware of the distinctive doctrines of Christianity, but they know that they want a better life than they are now living, and the message of Christianity offers a better life. We who are Christians and have a proper understanding of the gospel message, are commissioned and charged by Jesus Christ himself, to give the good news of salvation to those who are thirsty for water—the living water of eternal life. Verse 26 reads, then Jesus declared, "I who speak to you am He" (the Messiah). This woman was given an experience with Jesus and was now ready to accept Him as Messiah, Savior, and Lord. The woman then left her water jar, and went back to her town and said to the people, "Come see a man who told me everything I ever did. Could this be the Christ?" They came out of the town and made their way towards Jesus. This woman was changed from a social out-cast to a dedicated and effective missionary for the Lord Jesus Christ and the gospel of the kingdom of heaven. First John 1:9 states, "If we confess our sins, He is faithful and just to forgive us of our sins and cleanse us of all unrighteousness." The scriptures said that many of the Samaritans from that town believed Jesus because of the woman's testimony. "He told me everything I ever did." Outside of the Holy scriptures, our personal testimony of our relationship with Jesus Christ is the most powerful tool in the work of salvation. So when the Samaritans came to Him, they urged Him to stay with them, and He stayed two days. And because of Jesus' words many more became believers. They said to the woman, "We no longer believe just because of what you said; now we have heard for ourselves, and we know that this man really is the savior of the world." The divine grace of God that was extended to this social outcast and immoral woman was also extended by Jesus, to many people in the town in which the Samaritan woman lived.

In his famous classic, *My Utmost for His Highest*, the noted Christian author and evangelist Oswald Chambers made the following statement concerning the nature of divine grace and the converted life: "Eternal life is not a gift from God; eternal life is the gift of God. The energy and power which was so very evident in Jesus will be exhibited in us, by an act of the absolute sovereign grace of God, once we have made that complete and effective decision about sin. You shall receive power when the Holy Spirit has come upon you… (Acts 1:8), not power as a gift from the Holy Spirit, not something that He gives us. The life that was in Jesus becomes ours because of His cross, once we make the decision to be identified with him. If it is difficult to get right with God, it is because we refuse to make this moral decision about sin. But once we do decide, the full life of God comes in immediately. Jesus came to give us an endless supply of life, that you may be filled with all the fullness of God (Ephesians 3:19). Eternal life has nothing to do with time. It is the life which Jesus lived when He was down here, and the only source of life is the Lord Jesus Christ. Even the weakest saint can experience the power of the deity of the son of God, when he is willing to 'let go.' But any effort to 'hang on' to the least bit of our power will only diminish the life of Jesus in us. We have to keep letting go, and slowly, but surely, the great and full life of God will invade us, penetrating every part.

Then Jesus will have complete and effective dominion in us, and people will take notice that we have been with Him."

The story is told of a man, who having played several games of poker, lost a great deal of money to another man. He became so distraught, disappointed and angry, that he shot his opponent to death. The man was tried for murder. During the trial, letters of support poured in from everywhere asking for clemency for his life, because this man lived an exemplary life in the community, and this was his first and only crime. The judge was deeply moved and finally decided to pardon him for the crime. The judge wanted to tell the good news to the murderer himself, so he went to the prison, dressed like a clergyman. When he got to the prison cell, he told the prisoner that he brought him some good news. The prisoner refused to listen to the judge, in the garb (habit) of clergyman. He told the judge to get out and leave him alone to suffer his fate and die in the electric chair. Sadly, the judge turned away and left the man in prison. After the judge had long gone, the prisoner learned that he had turned his back on the judge and on a pardon that could have saved his life. The prisoner quickly wrote the judge a letter asking for another chance. After receiving the letter, the judge replied that he's not interested in the case anymore, that he had changed his mind and his pardon was revoked. Before dying in the electric chair, the man left a message. He said, "tell my family and friends that I didn't die in the electric chair because of the crime of murder. I died because I refused the pardon."

We don't have to die because we are sinners, Christ paid the penalty for us on Calvary's cross but we will perish because we rejected God's gracious mercy, forgiveness, grace and pardon. The mystery of divine grace is one of the greatest transactions this world has ever known, or will ever know. The Creator died for the creation. Christ took our sadness and offered us joy. He became a mortal human being, in order that we may become immortal beings of God. He suffered the judgement of God, so that we can enjoy the loving-kindness and tender mercies of the heavenly Father. The grace of God is a divine mystery! The human intellect cannot fully comprehend or fathom the length and breadth and depth of this mystery. The mystery of divine grace gives us some understanding of our value in the sight and economy of God. He loves us with an everlasting love! The following poem is an illustration of this truth:

"The Touch of the Master's Hand" by Myra Brooks.

> The Touch of the Master's Hand
> 'Twas battered and scarred, and the auctioneer
> Thought it scarcely worth his while
> To waste much time on the old violin,
> But held it up with a smile.
> "What am I bidden, good folks," he cried,
> "Who'll start the bidding for me?"
> "A dollar, a dollar. Then two! Only two?
> Two dollars, and who'll make it three?"
> "Three dollars, once; three dollars, twice;
> Going for three..."But no,
> From the room, far back, a grey-haired man
> Came forward and picked up the bow;
> Then wiping the dust from the old violin,
> And tightening the loosened strings,
> He played a melody pure and sweet,
> As a caroling angel sings.
> The music ceased, and the auctioneer,
> With a voice that was quiet and low,
> Said: "What am I bid for the old violin?"
> And he held it up with the bow.
> "A thousand dollars, and who'll make it two?
> Two thousand! And who'll make it three?
> Three thousand, once; three thousand, twice,
> And going and gone," said he.

The people cheered, but some of them cried,
"We do not quite understand.
What changed its worth?" Swift came the reply:
"The touch of the Master's hand."
And many a man with life out of tune,
And battered and scarred with sin,
Is auctioned cheap to the thoughtless crowd
Much like the old violin.
A "mess of pottage," a glass of wine,
A game — and he travels on.
He is "going" once, and "going" twice,
He's "going" and almost "gone."
But the Master comes, and the foolish crowd
Never can quite understand
The worth of a soul and the change that is
wrought
By the touch of the Master's hand.

God's divine grace provided salvation to lost humanity. God's grace empowers us to live above ungodliness and wordy passions. God's permissive and mysterious grace prepares us for the blessed hope of our Lord and Savior Jesus Christ. God's love is greater than all our sins. The grace of God is a divine mystery!

Chapter 8

The Journey Continues

"Those who know the Lord will trust Him because He rejects no one who comes to Him for help." —Psalm 9:10 (The Clear Word)

On June 29th 2010, Cindy and I attended the General Conference sessions of Seventh-day Adventists in Atlanta, Georgia. This was a deeply moving experience! We almost cancelled the trip because of a tennis accident that I sustained. We had already booked and paid for our hotel and flight reservations. I was barely able to walk because of a pinched nerve in my back. I had to use a crutch. I made regular visits to the chiropractor, had a complete CAT scan, powerful pain medication, physical therapy and special prayer at church. I had many sleepless nights because of the intense pain. By God's grace we were able to travel to the convention in Atlanta. The next day, Thursday July 1st, we visited the Georgia Aquarium. This was a most delightful experience. We then visited The Dr. Martin Luther King Center. This was also a very educational and beautiful event. For the next two days we attended General Conference meetings at the Georgia Dome. Because of a great deal of walking, I experienced a lot of pain in my lower back and right leg. I was able to get some relief by using a hand walker, pain medication and prayer. At the convention we encountered some old friends and made some new acquaintances.

In August of 2011, Cindy and I visited Cindy's side of the family in Berrien Springs, Michigan. Our purpose was to visit the whole family. We especially made the trip as a surprise for her mom's birthday on August 31st 2011. The entire Bullock family and in-laws took mom to Ponderosa restaurant in South Bend, Indiana. We contacted our son, Sean, on the telephone in San Francisco, California, and everyone took turns and spoke with him (we tried to confuse him by not telling him who he was talking with). We all had a delightful time!

In July 2012, I attended a convention in the Caribbean and visited with relatives and friends. Instead of staying in a hotel I made the decision to stay with some dear friends, the Maitlands, when I visited Trinidad. I attended church that weekend, and I was asked to preach the sermon. That was a challenge and a great honor. The Maitlands and I were invited out to dinner by relatives, and enjoyed a delightful visit. We traveled to different venues on the Island, did some shopping for souvenirs, and visited relatives and friends.

The next island on my itinerary was St. Vincent. Getting to that island was an experience that I will never forget. I flew from Trinidad to Barbados on my way to St. Vincent. While waiting at the International airport in Barbados, the passengers who were in transit to St. Vincent and beyond were told that our flight was delayed because of a tropical storm that developed. After waiting for many frustrating hours we were placed on a plane to St. Vincent. As we approached our destination our pilot was told that the storm had blown out all the lights on the island of St. Vincent. Instead of returning to Barbados immediately, he decided or was instructed to circle the area, waiting for the lights to be repaired. That was a very harrowing experience! After circling the area for about forty-five minutes, may passengers (including myself) became quite concerned about our safety! There we were, over the vast Atlantic Ocean. The night was black, no lights anywhere! We were circling round and round, waiting for the authorities to repair the lights at the airport on the island of St. Vincent. If that aircraft had lost power for any reason, we would had plunged into the ocean to certain death! The instructions were finally received to return to Barbados and to safety. Thanks be unto the Lord!

However we were not out of danger yet. Apparently, the go ahead was given to return to Barbados because we were running low on fuel. Now, the concern was, would there be enough fuel to get back to Barbados? There was a lot of chatter on the aircraft throughout the trip, but now there was only silence! Many people were praying and in deep contemplation! As we finally begin to approach the island of Barbados, people "began to breathe again". Apparently the fuel was very low because the aircraft was gliding just above the surface of the ocean! We made a safe landing thanks be unto our Lord in heaven! That night we waited for several more hours before another aircraft was provided to take us to our destination in St. Vincent. Everyone thought that the ordeal was finally over! That was not the case! Not very long after the small aircraft took off for our second attempt to reach St. Vincent, that we heard a terrible noise coming from the plane's engine. Once again the passengers became very concerned for our safety! However, after a tense two hours of travel that night, we finally landed at the airport in St. Vincent. Everyone was tired, exhausted but relieved and thankful to our Lord and Father in heaven for His loving kindness and tender mercies!

The next day, I continued my journey by boat to Union Islands. This island was part of the island nation of St. Vincent and the Grenadines. One of my sisters and a few other relatives resided on this island. I stayed in one of their houses, with one of our brothers and his wife. The purpose of the convention was to highlight and promote the many educational, cultural and social aspects of the island of St. Vincent and the Grenadines. The convention planners sponsored many social programs and activities for those in attendance.

The cultural and social programs in which I was most interested were the fashion show, the island cruise, the beach party, and the family get together (reunion). The fashion show featured many styles from the past, present, and future. The presentations were informal, contemporary, and formal. I did not personally experience a yacht cruise of the islands, but I was told that the sights were breathtaking and the event was exhilarating. The beach party that I attended was a memorable event! I met some acquaintances and made some friends! The water was warm and delightful! The meal that was prepared was delicious! The Caribbean music enhanced the entire occasion with the magic of rhythm and song! Many family members from the United States, Canada and the United Kingdom made the trip to Union Island, St. Vincent for the occasion. We had a small family reunion. This was a wonderful experience. It was a joy to see relatives that I haven't seen for several years. I met relatives that I'd never seen before, and did not know I had. This was truly a heart-warming experience! We attended church on the week end before leaving for our various destinations. Many family members, myself included, took part in a choir that was formed for the special event. We practiced and sang to the glory of the Lord! As was requested of me, I preached the sermon for the Sunday night service! I trust that many received a blessing! I had a pleasant and safe trip back home to the United States.

On March 14th, 2013, Cindy and I traveled to England to attend my niece's wedding. After travelling through London by train we finally arrived at our destination safely. Our host was a gentle, elderly Christian lady, by the name of Mrs. Annis Mahbear. March 16th, the day before the wedding, was Cindy's birthday. I had planned to take her out to dinner and visit some sites in London, but because of the inclement weather (it rained all day), we had a quiet celebration at the residence in which we were staying. On March 17th we drove to the SDA church for the wedding ceremony. Everything was beautiful, except the bride (my niece) got stuck in London traffic. The time of the waiting were some anxious moments indeed! However, this time provided an opportunity for people to acquaint themselves with other attendees from Canada, the Caribbean, the United States and different parts of the

My Journey of Discovery

United Kingdom. The bride and the bridal party finally arrived at the church, and the wedding ceremony proceeded as planned!

After the wedding pictures were taken, we all drove to another venue in London for the reception. The catered dining was truly exquisite. The decorations were colorful and elegant. Many well-wishers were called upon to give their recollections regarding the bride and groom. When I was called upon to speak, I gave remarks of recommendation about Neachea, my niece (I did not know her husband) and asked the Lord's blessings on both of them and on their life together. On Tuesday, March 19, we took a taxi to London Heathrow international airport. This was our first real experience with London traffic during this trip. I've been in many traffic jams, and the traffic situation we encountered in London compared well with some of the worst traffic patterns that I've seen. In spite of the nerve racking experience, the Lord helped us to get to the airport in time to catch our flight back to the United States. We had a long and beautiful flight, and arrived home safely.

In May 2014, Cindy and I drove to Williamsburg, Virginia, to celebrate our 40th wedding anniversary (May 20th 2014). This was a promotional venture, involving a timeshare. After attending the necessary two hour meetings, we were free to celebrate our wedding anniversary. We spent four days and three nights in Williamsburg and visited historic sights. The Lord helped us find our hotel! The timeshare company paid for two nights of our hotel stay and we paid for one additional night.

On September 12th, Cindy was admitted to Carroll County Hospital Center because of severe chest pains. After tests, blood work, EKG, and ultrasounds were done, the attending physician determined that gallbladder surgery had to be done. The surgery was done on Saturday, September 13, 2014. On Sunday night Cindy spiked a high fever. As a result of this development she was kept an extra day in the hospital. More blood work was done and she was given antibiotics by I.V. method. She was discharged from the hospital in the afternoon, on Monday 15 September, 2014.

The Journey Continues

Cindy regained full capacity and returned to work after a period of recuperation. We thanked the Lord for His goodness and His loving kindness!

An unfortunate situation developed as a result of the aforementioned surgical procedure. The surgery costs over $20,000. The insurance company, Blue Cross/Blue Shield, refused to pay Cindy's hospital bill. We had a crisis on our hands! We took the matter to the Lord in prayer and we also asked our fellow church members to remember us in their prayers. We appealed the matter and sent the following letter to Blue Cross/Blue Shield insurance company.

> 10/1/2014
> Dear Dr. Glen Heise:
> This letter is in response to your letter dated 9/22/2014. I, Cynthia M. Edwards, have visited my physicians, Stephen J. Silorski, MD, and Nilar U., MD, at Carroll Primary Care, for chest pains on more than one occasion. On the evening of September 11th, 2014, I had to leave work at Carroll Lutheran Village (I work there part time) with severe chest pains. I managed to drive the short distance home safely. This was about 7:30 p.m. on Thursday, September 11th. Because the doctor's office was closed for the day, I did not want to go to the emergency room without my doctor's approval and authorization. I took Bayer aspirin for the pain, and made it through the night. At 8 a.m. on Friday, September 12th, my husband called Carroll Primary Care and spoke to the nurse by the name of Barbara. My husband told her that I needed to see the doctor immediately, owing to the intense chest and back pains I was having. After consulting with the physician, the nurse told my husband that "there is no

point brining your wife to the doctor's office—you must take her to the emergency room at Carroll Hospital Center, and I will notify the ER of your arrival." My husband drove me to the hospital and we arrived at the ER at about 11:00 a.m. I could not walk. I was taken in by wheelchair because the pain was severe. An IV was started and blood work was taken. An EKG/ECG, ultrasound, and other tests were done. From physical symptoms and the clinical tests that were done, the emergency room physician determined that I had an infected gall bladder. He sent for the attending surgeon, S. Chanarong, MD. I was admitted to the hospital. The doctor told my husband and me that I will be scheduled for gall bladder surgery at 7:30 a.m. on Saturday, September 13th, 2014. The procedure took place as scheduled. The surgeon, Dr. S. Chanarong, spoke to my husband in the recovery room. He said that I should be discharged on Sunday, September 14th. He also told my husband that my gall bladder was very infected. Saturday night I spiked a high fever, and the doctor decided to keep me another day in the hospital. More blood work was done and I was given antibiotics by IV. Monday 15th September the high fever decreased, and I was discharged from the hospital that afternoon.

    Dr. Glen Heise, I have worked for fifteen (15) years at Weis Markets, and I've paid my health insurance premiums faithfully all this time. If at a time like this, I cannot use my health insurance, what was the point and purpose for paying health insurance premiums for all these years? Dr. Glen Heise, to deny the payment of this hospital bill is wrong, unfair and unjust. My husband is retired and we're struggling to survive. We do not have the financial resources to pay this hospital bill. In spite of the intense chest and back pain, I would not have had this surgery, if I knew that Capital Blue Cross would not pay this bill. I plead with you to honor this obligation and liquidate this hospital bill. Thank you

    Sincerely,
    Cynthia M. Edwards

Our appeal was granted, and the entire hospital bill was paid, except for about $2,000 that we had to pay out of our pocket. We thanked the Lord for His kindness and His tender mercies towards us.

Chapter 9
A Joyful Celebration

"My deliverance has been like feasting in your presence. My lips are eager to joyfully sing your praises." —Psalms 63:5 (The Clear Word)

Cindy and I decided to revisit Hawaii with two purposes in mind. First, we wanted to visit our son Sean who lives in Maui, Hawaii, whom we hadn't seen for about 3 years, since he left home "to make his mark in the world." Second, we wanted to celebrate our 41st wedding anniversary.

After vacation time for Cindy and Eliot were secured from their respective places of employment, we purchased two return airline tickets from United Air Lines, a month in advance of our departure date to Hawaii. We also made the following preparations: we e-mailed our itinerary to our son Sean, reserved a rental car with Hertz Rental Cars, and we went to the post office and placed a hold on our mail for the duration of our vacation. On Tuesday, May 12th, Cindy and I left our home at 2:45 a.m. and caught our flight that departed from Baltimore-Washington International Airport at 6:01 a.m. for Los Angeles, California. We had an uneventful and beautiful flight to LAX. We were tired of all the preparations that had to be made, therefore we slept almost all the way to Los Angeles, California.

About a week before we made our trip to Hawaii, I had a dream about our trip. In my dream, Cindy and I were at a large airport in California. We were in the process of transferring to our flight to Maui, Hawaii. After waiting at the airport for a while, we finally boarded the aircraft. While waiting in the aircraft for de-

A Joyful Celebration

parture, we discovered that we were on the wrong plane. We disembarked, and after some negotiation, we were able to get on the right plane, that took us safely to our destination in Hawaii. I told Cindy the dream, but attached no special significance to it.

During the actual trip, we arrived at LAX as scheduled, for the last leg of our trip to Hawaii. To our great surprise, we encountered a situation that was similar in many ways to the events that transpired in my dream. At the airport in Los Angeles, Cindy and I boarded the aircraft, and took our assigned seats for the remainder of our trip to Hawaii. No sooner than we were seated, a couple came down the aisle of the plane and said "We think you're in our seats"! After checking our tickets, we discovered that we had the same seat numbers as this couple. After consulting the flight attendant, Cindy and I were reassigned to two seats in another part of the aircraft. The seat assignments of other passengers were mixed up as well. One man almost got into a fist fight with one of the flight attendants because he could not be seated with his wife and family in the same row. The confused situation occurred when the aircraft that was originally assigned for this particular flight, was changed because repairs had to be done to the plane. The original aircraft was replaced with a smaller plane. This led to the frustration and confusion that ensued. The situation was finally resolved, and we continued our flight to our destination to Maui, Hawaii. We thanked the Lord Jesus for His goodness.

After the five-and-half-hour flight from Los Angeles International Airport (LAX) we landed at Kahului airport in Maui, Hawaii, on Tuesday, the 12th of May. We were met by our son Sean. After picking up our rental car, we followed him to his house in Kihei, Maui. The drive took 30 to 45 minutes. Because of our long flight we rested for the rest of the day. The next day, Cindy and I were introduced to the other residents of the house. Later that morning, Sean accompanied Cindy and me to the Foodland grocery store, where we purchased many food items for our meals during our visit in Maui. On Thursday May 14th Sean, Cheyenne

My Journey of Discovery

(Sean's girlfriend), her son Isaiah (7 years old), Cindy and I drove for about one hour from the city of Kihei to the city of Lahaina. After visiting different shopping malls and purchasing some items, the time came to attend the main event of that day, the Luau, a traditional Hawaiian feast. This was truly a delightful experience. The dinner was held outside in an open garden, under the starry skies, by the sea. In the distance across the waters we were enraptured by a breathtaking and picturesque sunset. The setting was enhanced as the sea kissed the ocean. The method of service was buffet style. There were two long lines. The menu consisted of pina colada and several other alcoholic beverages. Some of the dishes that were served were poi (a potato-like root), Poke Ahi (tuna), Poke He'e (Octopus), Luau Kalo (taro leaf stew), Eylua (sweet potato), Pipi ko'ala (grilled beef steak), chicken, long rice, Moa (Island style chicken), I'a (main style fish), stir fry vegetables, local style fried rice, pot hole salad (fern shoot and Maui onions mixed with tomatoes), Lomilomi salmon (local tomatoes, onions, and salted salmon), freshly baked Hawaiian sweet bread rolls, banana bread and haupia, local grown green salad, fresh island fruit and assorted island desserts. The weather cooperated perfectly. The temperature was about 75 to 80 degrees. Balmy sea breezes from the ocean enhanced the ambience of the evening. This was truly a delightful occasion. On Friday, May 15th, we went shopping and spent the rest of the day visiting the rain forest at Haleokala National Park. Elevations in the park range from sea level to 10,023 feet at the summit of Puukukui. Among the park's wildlife is Hawaii's state bird, the rare nene (Hawaii's goose). The weather can change rapidly at high elevations on Haleakala.

Temperatures usually range between 35 to 70 degrees Fahrenheit, but can be below freezing at anytime of the year when the wind chill factor is taken into account. Intense sunlight, thick clouds, heavy rains and high winds can happen daily.

A Joyful Celebration

On Saturday May 16th, we attended the Seventh-day Adventist church in the city of Kahululi. The service was quite inspiring. In his sermon for the day, the speaker spoke of Christ first coming to the earth. Many of His own people were unprepared and unsure whether He was the promised Messiah. They asked Him if He was the anointed one, or should they look for someone else. The speaker pointed out that in the same way that many people were unprepared for His first coming, in a similar way, many believers will be unprepared for His second coming also. At lunchtime there was a fellowship dinner for all who wanted to stay. Present at the table, where my wife and I were sitting, were an evangelist and his wife, who were visiting Hawaii from California, and two other ministers who were also visiting from other states. Our conversation concerned issues of a spiritual nature. This was a most engaging and enjoyable experience.

On the evening of May 16, we drove to the seaside town of Lahaina. From there we departed on a two hour excursion at sea. This included narration by a trained naturalist. We enjoyed a sunset dinner and cocktail cruise. The Hawaiian sunset are among the most breath-taking we have ever seen. This was truly a memorable occasion. The next day, Sunday, we did some shopping and spent the rest of the day at the beach. On Monday 18th, May, we visited the shopping mall in the city of Kahului. Later that evening we attended a variety and cultural performance that featured Hawaiian history and culture through traditional arts, music, and dance.

Wednesday, May 20th, was a special day! Cindy and I were married 41 years ago. All of us—Cindy, Sean, Cheyenne, Corey, Lena and I—spent all morning and part of the afternoon at the beach. There were many people at the beach, although it was not crowded. I entered the water and started enjoying myself. The water was warm and delightful! The other members of the group choose to stay on the beach and sun bathe, rather than enter the water. I encountered some high school students who were swimming! They were on a school outing to the beach. As I swam, I mixed and mingled with the students. "Does everyone in this group go to the same high school?" I asked one of the young men.

"Yes," he responded, with some hesitation. They were playing with two or three different sized balls. I caught one of the balls, as a student threw it in my direction, and joined in the fun.

"Did any teachers or parents accompany the students on the bus, to the beach?" I asked the student.

"Only three or four teachers came with us," replied one young lady. As she said this, I looked in the direction of the shore, and we saw the large charter bus that was parked on the street that ran along the shoreline. Not all of the students were in the water—some were on the beach, enjoying the sunshine. Others were playing volley ball and still others were dancing to Hawaiian music. After playing catch-ball with the students for a while, one female student asked, "what state are you from?"

"Maryland" I said.

She continued, "did you come to Hawaii on vacation or to live?" I responded, "My wife and I came to Hawaii on vacation for our wedding anniversary and to visit our son, who lives in Maui". All of the students were welcoming and friendly. This event was a beautiful experience.

We drove home, took a shower and prepared ourselves to attend a dinner invitation. Corey and Lena, a couple who lived in the same house in which our son Sean resided, invited Cindy and I out to dinner, to celebrate our wedding anniversary. We were pleasantly surprised and delighted. They took us to a restaurant called Pita Palace. Pita is an Italian bread that is served in many ways with different dishes. As we entered the restaurant, we were taken to our seats by a well attired waiter. We took our seats at a dinner table that was square and nicely set with beautiful silverware. "This is one of the most popular eating places in the city of Kihei, and it's our favorite place to eat," Corey said, "We usually come here for special events," he added. This occasion served as an opportunity to get acquainted with our new friends.

"Lena, Cindy and I would like to thank you for cutting her hair, two days ago" I said.

"You're very welcome, I was glad to do it", she responded. The waiter brought our drinks, non-alcoholic pina colada and a salad.

"My ex-husband and our son and daughter live in Seattle, Washington. I would like to bring them here to Hawaii, to live with me," Lena commented. She also informed us that her parents moved to the United States from Vietnam, while she was still a little girl. Cindy and I were pleased to know that Corey was from our home state of Maryland.

"I attended Howard University Law School, but I didn't finish owing to family and academic difficulties," Corey said. As we were talking, the waiter served our main course dinner. Cindy and I ordered a fish plater, with tartar dressing, seasoned rice, stir fry vegetables, and seasoned pita bread. Corey and Lena had the grilled beef steak dinner, marinated vegetables, seasoned Hawaiian rice, and garlic pita bread. Cindy and I shared with our guests some highlights of our first meeting. I began the story. "We both worked at the Andrews University bindery in Berrien Springs, Michigan. One day I saw Cindy and said "hi," she paid no attention to me, nor did she respond to my greeting. The next day, she passed by the place I was working and said, "Hi, I'm sorry for ignoring you yesterday." I accepted her apology. After that meeting, we became more acquainted as time passed.

We had a sumptuous dinner, and no one wanted dessert. We returned home, and Cindy and I made preparations for our long journey home the next day.

On the morning of Thursday, May 21st, we drove to Kahului Airport (OGG) and returned the rental car. We had a beautiful and uneventful 5-hour flight to Los Angeles international airport (LAX). We successfully made our connecting flight to Houston, Texas. Our time in Houston was noteworthy and eventful. After everyone boarded the aircraft for our final destination to Baltimore/Thurgood Marshall International Airport (BWI), we were told that there was a problem with the plane's heating system. Rather than disembark or cancelling the flight, everyone was kept on the aircraft, while the heating system was repaired. The process took about 3-1/4 hours. Many people became frustrated and upset because of this inconvenience, especially those who would miss their connecting flight at BWI. We arrived at our final destination at 7:24 Friday morning of May 22nd, 2015. We arrived safely home in Westminster, Maryland, even though we were very tired and worn out. We thank and praise the Lord for His loving kindness and His tender mercies.

    When Cindy and I returned from our vacation in Hawaii, we were informed that Cindy's dad, Frank Bullock, was becoming worse and his cancer treatment was not successful. At his request, Cindy and I visited mom and dad while they were still alive. Dad wanted to be anointed. I had the privilege of taking part in anointing both mom (she had Alzheimer's disease) and dad. Dad lost his battle with cancer and went to meet the Lord. Mom grieved and mourned for her husband. On October 10, 2015, Natalie Bullock passed away at home with her family by her side. My family and I had the privilege of taking part in the funeral services. After the burial service we all attended a beautiful dinner event.

Chapter 10
Calvary: The Greatest Miracle

"There is therefore now no condemnation to those who are in Christ Jesus, who do not walk according to the flesh, but according to the spirit" —Romans 8:1.

As indicated by the above passage of scripture, those believers who fully accept and believe in the life, death and resurrection of Jesus, and live according to the guidance of the holy spirit, are acceptable and pleasing to God. This reality was made possible by the death and resurrection of Jesus Christ.

I choose to conclude this book by asking and examining the question: were we at the cross, when Jesus was crucified? The passage in the gospel of Luke chapter 23, verses 17-25, described the events that transpired before the crucifixion of Jesus. When I read this passage of scripture, the question that occurred to me was, "what was going through Barabbas' mind?" The history of this man is limited, according to what was recorded about him in the gospels. We know very little about him prior to his fateful encounter with Pilate and Jesus, that Passover Friday. We know that he was part of an insurrection. In other words, he rebelled and revolted against the Roman authority. We know that he was sentenced to death for his crime. Another interesting point about Barabbas is that some manuscripts of the Bible say that his first name may actually have been Jesus. So, coincidently, his full name would have been Jesus Barabbas, or Jesus, son of the father, which is what Barabbas means. I thought about what may have transpired

My Journey of Discovery

in Barabbas' mind in the hours leading up to his historic meeting with Jesus. We seem to know the thoughts of everyone else—the Pharisees, the disciples, Pontius Pilate, Joseph and Nicodemus, even the Roman centurion. But we know nothing about the thoughts of Barabbas. As I read the above passage of scripture, I wondered what Barabbas might have been thinking. I wish to look at Jesus' crucifixion from Barabbas' perspective. The pen of inspiration tells us to use our imagination "to grasp each scene" of the last moments of Christ's life.

    Let us imagine that it is the morning of the sixth day of the week in the year AD 31. Barabbas wakes up in his dark, dingy, cold damp dungeon-like cell. His body is chilled to the bone. As he rises from the cold floor that he slept on for the past few weeks, the dungeon of the Roman Prefect, Pontius Pilate, has been his home. This only human contact that Barabbas has had in recent days was that of the Roman soldiers. Most likely, these visits were not warm fuzzy visits. The only light that Barabbas probably saw was that of the lantern that lit the hallway outside his cell. It seems like years ago since the insurrection took place. Barabbas remembers the moment that he struck that Roman solider dead. It all seems like a bad dream now. He became angry about the trial he received. It all took place so fast! It all seemed like a blur. The only thing he remembered with crystal clear clarity, was the pronouncement of his sentence, crucify him! Barabbas had waited in his cell since that moment, and now the day had arrived! Today he will die! Today, Barabbas will be crucified, for the crime of murder and insurrection. How ironic that his crucifixion should coincide with the Passover! Certainly, the curse of death will not pass over Barabbas' house today, as it did for the Jews in Egypt! He was a doomed man! Barabbas began to think back on his life. He realized that all his life he had been a rebel, causing trouble and stirring up problems for himself and others. And now, this was the result of his bad choices. He had no freedom, no dignity, no future, no hope! All because he was a rebel. All because he had focused on what he could do! Barabbas had claimed to be the Messiah! He thought he could save himself by the things he could do, as a national revolutionary leader. Many people believed in him. He actually had a following for a little while. He thought that his way could save not only himself, but others from the oppression of the Roman empire. He thought that he could deliver himself and whoever wanted to follow him from the iron grip of Rome. He thought he could be his own Messiah! He was wrong!

In her book, *Man of Destiny*, pp. 645, 646, Ellen G. White made the following statement: "It was customary at this feast to release some one prisoner whom the people might choose. This custom was of pagan invention; there was not a shadow of justice in it, but it was greatly prized by the Jews. The Roman authorities at this time held a prisoner named Barabbas who was under sentence of death. This man claimed to be the Messiah. He claimed authority to establish a different order of things, to set the world right. Under satanic delusion he claimed that whatever he could obtain by theft and robbery was his own. He had done wonderful things through satanic agencies, he had gained a following among the people, and had excited sedition against the Roman government. Under cover of religious enthusiasm, he was a hardened and desperate villain, bent on rebellion and cruelty." Now, there was Barabbas staring death right in the face. Several cells down from his cell, two of Barabbas followers, also sat face to face with death. It was all Barabbas' fault. His words convinced them. They followed his lead. They hung on to his every word. Barabbas can feel their blood on his hands. But there is no relief for this sinner. He thinks to himself, "if you are the Messiah, get out of this one, and save your friends also." He came to the most stunning and humbling realization! He can't save anyone! But worst of all, he can't save himself either! All he can do is wait to die the death that he rightly deserved.

Then all of a sudden his thoughts were interrupted. Roman centurions rushed through the dungeon door. Could his wait for death be over already? They violently grabbed Barabbas and dragged him to his feet. He fought back with all his might. If they are about to kill him, he will not go easy. Surrender had never been one of Barabbas strong qualities, and he was not about to change! He kicked, he punched, he screamed! But it was all for naught, despite his best efforts and struggles to save himself. Finally the guards restrained him. They dragged him out of his cell and towards Pilate's court.

As the darkness of his dungeon opened up into the light of a beautiful spring morning, Barabbas realized that it had been several days since he felt the warmth of the sunlight on his face. The rank smell of the dungeon disappeared and the scent of a spring morning filled his senses. He enjoyed the moment, but the moment was short lived. He realized a bone chilling reality. This is the last time, the last time, he will feel the sunshine on his face! The last time the sweet smell of the spring air will fill his nose and lungs! He knew that very soon, the pleasant feel of that sunlight will be replaced by the excruciating pain of spikes, nailed through his hands and feel. The wonderful smell of springtime will soon be replaced by the horrifying stench of death. Barabbas realized that he was a dead man—dead in sins and transgressions. There was no hope for him! This murderer, thief, and rebel would now suffer the fate he most certainly deserves.

Barabbas' thoughts were again interrupted—this time by the sights and sounds of a riotous crowd. Their yelling was incomprehensible. Barabbas saw the mob, and with disdain thought to himself, "what a pitiful bunch, they're anxious to see me die." Then he saw Pontius Pilate, the same man who sentenced him to death. Barabbas thought to himself, "what more does he want with me? He already sentenced me to death. Does he want to watch me suffer for a while before my crucifixion?" But then, Barabbas looked past Pilate. He noticed a man in intense pain. The man was barely able to stand up on his feet. It was obvious that he had been beaten—nearly to death. Parts of his beard were yanked out, seemingly from the root. His face was bloodied and swollen from punches. Blood seemed to cover his entire body. Barabbas thought, "What did he do to deserve this?" As Barabbas continued to look at the man, their eyes met. The man's eyes pierced Barabbas to his very heart. Barabbas suddenly recognized the man now. "That is Jesus of Nazareth, what was he doing here?" Barabbas thought, "He's such a goody two shoes. Why would he be in trouble?" Barabbas remembered Jesus' preaching. love your enemies and blessed are the meek for they shall inherit the earth! Obviously, his enemies didn't love him. There was certainly no blessing for his meekness. Barabbas was confused, and wondered what could Jesus have done to deserve the beating and the treatment he received. Barabbas knew that many people thought that Jesus was the Messiah! He had seen some of Jesus' healings! He heard the news that a man was raised after being dead for four days. He heard Jesus preached with an authority that seemed to come from God.

    Barabbas did not agree with Jesus' philosophy or with his methods. Barabbas knew that Jesus would do nothing that would deserve the treatment he received, and definitely nothing that was worthy of death. Yet, there they both stood! As Barabbas continued to look at Jesus, perhaps, some pity crept into his hardened heart. Perhaps, for just a brief moment, Barabbas thought to himself, "I deserve this punishment, but he does not." Jesus stood there, making no complaints, not angry, not fighting back. Jesus stood there with a serene and noble countenance and dignified bearing. Barabbas again thought, "how can he be in the same predicament that I am in?" His thoughts were interrupted by Pilate's voice. The historic words are recorded in Matthew 27:17. This verse of scripture, in many Greek manuscripts, reads the following way: "Whom do you want me to release for you? Jesus Barabbas or Jesus who is called Christ?" The brief moment of pity that Barabbas may have experienced, was replaced by excitement! Barabbas thought, "I have a chance to be set free and escape death." But again, Barabbas looked over at Jesus. Despite his battered body, Barabbas saw very clearly the innocence and the purity in Jesus' form and bearing. As he stood next to Jesus, Barabbas realized that he was a hardened, wicked, and depraved sinner. Barabbas thought, "if I could see the contrast between this man and myself, it should be much more obvious to these people." Then suddenly Barabbas heard his name being shouted. He turned to look and he realized that the crowd was shouting his name. They had chosen him, over Jesus! How could this be!

Then Pilate spoke the words recorded in Matthew 27:22. "Then what shall I do with the Jesus who is called Christ?" Barabbas heard the response, but he could not believe his ears! "Crucify him!" "Crucify him!" The same penalty that had been given to Barabbas, would now be given to Jesus of Nazareth. How could this be? How could the crowd choose Barabbas over Jesus? How could they choose a murderer, over a healer, a thief, over a giver of life, a rebel, over a peacemaker? In her classic best seller, *Desire of Ages*, pp. 646, 647, Ellen G. White states: "Jesus was taken, faint with weariness and covered with wounds, and scourged in the sight of the multitude. And the solider led him away into the hall, called Praetorian: and they call together the whole band. And they clothed him with purple, and platted a crown of thorns, and put it about his head, and began to salute him. Hail, king of the Jews! And they…did spit upon him, and bowing their knees worshiped him. Occasionally some wicked hand snatched the reed that had been placed in his hand, and struck the crown upon his brow, forcing the thorns into his temple, and sending the blood trickling down his face and beard. Wonder, O heavens! and be astonished, o earth! Behold the oppressor and the oppressed. A maddened throng enclosed the savior of the world. Mocking and jeering are mingled with the course of oaths and blasphemy. His lowly birth and humble life are commented upon by the unfeeling mob. His

Calvary: The Greatest Miracle

claim to be the Son of God is ridiculed and a vulgar jest and insulting sneer are passed from lip to lip. Satan led the cruel mob in its abuse of the savior. It was his purpose to provoke him to retaliation if possible, or drive him to perform a miracle to release himself, and thus break up the plan of salvation. One stain upon his human life, one failure of his humanity to endure the terrible test, and the Lamb of God would have been an imperfect offering, and the redemption of man a failure. But he who by a command could bring the heavenly host to his aid, he could have driven that mob in terror from his sight by the flashing of his divine majesty, submitted with perfect calmness to the coarsest insult and outrage."

The biblical record is silent about what became of Barabbas. We don't know anything more about him. It would seem likely that Barabbas could have been a spectator at Calvary. That was most likely the big event that day. He probably saw Jesus nailed to a cross that was intended for him. He probably saw Jesus receiving ridicule that should have been directed at him! And he probably saw Jesus suffered the death that most definitely should have been his death. As I reflected on this scene, I wondered why the biblical record was silent about what happened to this man, Barabbas. Then an amazing thought occurred to me, that caused chills to run up and down my spine! I am Barabbas! You are Barabbas! Every sinner is Barabbas!

The death that Jesus died was my death! The ridicule he received, was my ridicule! The crown of thorns that Jesus wore, that was my crown! Most definitely, the cross on which Jesus was nailed, was my cross! The truth is, I am Barabbas! Yes, I was at the cross when Jesus was crucified! And so was every Christian believer! The apostle Paul gave us good news in Romans 5:8, he states, "but God demonstrates his own love towards us, in that while we were yet sinners, Christ died for us." Yes, Jesus died on Barabbas' cross! The reason the bible record is silent about Barabbas' future and what became of him is because each Christian believer have the opportunity to complete Barabbas' story!

In Galatians chapter 2, verse 20, the apostle Paul states: "I have been crucified with Crist, it is no longer I who live, but Christ lives in me; and the life which I now live in the flesh I live by faith in the son of God, who loved me and gave himself for me." In his book, *My Utmost for His Highest*, Oswald Chambers states: "The inescapable spiritual need each of us have, is the need to sign the death certificate of our sin nature. I must take my emotional opinions and intellectual beliefs and be willing to turn them into a moral verdict against the nature of sin: that is, any claim I have to my right to myself. Paul said, "I have been crucified with Christ…" He did not say, "I have made a determination to imitate Jesus Christ," or "I will really make an effort to follow him; I have been identified with him in his death." Once I reach this moral decision and act on it, all that Christ accomplished for us on the cross is accomplished in me. My unrestrained commitment of myself to God gives the Holy Spirit the opportunity to grant to me the holiness of Jesus Christ. "… it is no longer I who live…" My individuality remains, but my primary motivations for living and the nature that rules me are radically changed. I have the same human body, but the old satanic right to myself has been destroyed" and the life which I now live in the flesh, "not the life which I long to live, but the life I now live is my mortal flesh—the life which others can see," I live by faith in the son of God. "This faith was not Paul's own faith in Jesus Christ, but the faith in the son, God had given to him (Ephesians 2:8). It is no longer a faith, but a faith that transcends all imaginable limits…a faith that comes only from the son of God." Jesus died on the cross that was meant for us! Let us all accept God's free gift of salvation that was made possible by Jesus' death on the cross at Calvary. Amen!

We invite you to view the complete
selection of titles we publish at:
www.ASPECTBooks.com

We encourage you to write us
with your thoughts about this,
or any other book we publish at:
info@ASPECTBooks.com

ASPECT Books' titles may be purchased in
bulk quantities for educational, fund-raising,
business, or promotional use.
bulksales@ASPECTBooks.com

Finally, if you are interested in seeing
your own book in print, please contact us at:
publishing@ASPECTBooks.com

We are happy to review your manuscript at no charge.

www.ingramcontent.com/pod-product-compliance
Lightning Source LLC
Chambersburg PA
CBHW071624170426
43195CB00038B/2114